LIVING SKILLS FOR MENTALLY HANDICAPPED PEOPLE

THERAPY IN PRACTICE

Series Editor: Jo Campling

This series of books is aimed at 'therapists' concerned with rehabilitation in a very broad sense. The intended audience particularly includes occupational therapists, physiotherapists and speech therapists, but many titles will also be of interest to nurses, psychologists, medical staff, social workers, teachers or volunteer workers. Some volumes will be interdisciplinary, others aimed at one particular profession. All titles will be comprehensive but concise, and practical but with due reference to relevant theory and evidence. They are not research monographs but focus on professional practice, and will be of value to both students and qualified personnel.

Living Skills for Mentally Handicapped People

Christine Peck,

Head Occupational Therapist,
Chace Village Mental Handicap Unit,
Chase Farm Hospital,
Enfield, Middlesex.

and

Chia Swee Hong,

Senior Occupational Therapist,
Occupational Therapy Department,
Hales Hospital,
Norwich.

CROOM HELM
London & Sydney

© 1988 Christine Peck and Chia Swee Hong
Croom Helm Ltd, Provident House,
Burrell Row, Beckenham, Kent BR3 1AT

Croom Helm Australia, 44–50 Waterloo Road,
North Ryde, 2113, New South Wales

British Library Cataloguing in Publication Data

Peck, Christine
  Living skills for mentally handicapped
  people. — (Therapy in practice)
  1. Mentally handicapped —
  Rehabilitation
  I. Title   II. Hong, Chia Swee   II Series
  362.3′8   HV3004
  ISBN 0–7099–4057–2

Distributed exclusively in the USA and non-exclusively in Canada by
Paul H. Brookes Publishing Co., Post Office Box 10624, Baltimore,
Maryland 21285–0624.

Filmset by Mayhew Typesetting, Bristol, England
Printed and bound in Great Britain
by Billing & Sons Limited, Worcester.

Contents

Acknowledgements

Although every effort has been made, it is not possible to trace or contact all sources of material reproduced in this book, and we therefore regret any inadvertent omission of acknowledgement where it is due. We would particularly like to thank the Toy Libraries Association for allowing us to reproduce a chapter from the *Good Toy Guide* 1982, and to Sheila Wolfendale and Trevor Bryans for their 'Guidelines for Teachers' No. 1.

We would also like the thank the following people who, through their help, co-operation, experience and/or written information (from courses we have attended) have been of considerable assistance to us in writing this book. They are Dr Karel and Mrs Bertha Bobath, Walli Meier, Sophie Levete, Veronica Sherbourne, Peter Wilcock, Sheena Wickings and Jo Campling. Enfield Health Authority have also provided very tangible support.

Many colleagues have also helped. These include Julie Cater, Beryl Upson, Joanna Barnes, Claire Blundy, Gladys Walker, Andrew Kelly, Audrey White, Maureen Crawt, Julia Middleton, Gill Pointer, Janet Hill, Anni Hogg, Joyce Hawkins, Angela Pinnuck, Heather Ferguson, Jenny Green, Christine Robinson and Patricia Ward.

We are indebted to those who showed great dedication in either reading or producing the manuscript (or both!) i.e. Ben Sacks, Chris Roberts, Linda Furner, Vivien Bower, Doreen Carter and Sheena Wickings (again!). Particular thanks go to Frank Bayford for his wonderful illustrations, and to Sue Oakley for her help and dedication in producing the final manuscript(s)!!

And finally, thanks to our families and friends, who have given us much-needed support, and to the people who live in Chace Village, Enfield, Middlesex, who taught us so much.

Foreword

In recent years there has been a plethora of writings about training people who have a mental handicap, and most of these are concerned with the type of service thought suitable for them and their families. No group is more heterogeneous than people who have a mental handicap, and the services required by them must cover a correspondingly wide range, in terms of living situations, specific services and the training needed to help them develop their full potential.

It cannot be sufficiently emphasised that many aspects of the training needed are technical in nature, and that the people carrying out the training need expertise in a large number of specific skills. However, technical skills alone are not sufficient; staff also have to show positive and supportive attitudes to a wide range of issues in order to meet client needs. Many of these needs can only be met by specialists in particular fields, but the need to work towards a general improvement in living skills and independence can be met by everyone involved.

Teaching people to become more independent is the responsibility of everyone involved in training. Suggestions for developing independent living skills form a large part of this book, and deal with most of the things that *actually have to be done*. Helping people to live better lives is a worthy aim for any professional. This book makes a real contribution to this area.

Dr B.I. Sacks
Formerly Consultant Psychiatrist, Chace Village, Enfield.
Currently Professor in Mental Handicap,
Charing Cross Hospital, London.

Preface

People who have a mental handicap have a range of special needs in many different areas, e.g. physical function, learning and understanding, social skills, communication and independent living skills. They may also have additional needs that are not directly caused by their mental handicap, e.g. cerebral palsy, epilepsy, sensory deficits or mental illness. This makes each client unique in their training needs, and requires those involved in meeting those needs to have sufficient skill and flexibility to adopt whichever approach (or combination of approaches) brings most benefit to the client.

There are many theoretical books available which describe various aspects of mental handicap, and even more books describing the use of specific techniques and activities, but there are very few that link together the theory and the training activities to provide a basic approach to planning and implementing therapeutic programmes. This book, which is directed primarily towards students and newly qualified practitioners who have some knowledge of basic human development and who want to work with people who have mental/multiple handicaps, aims to unite theoretical and practical aspects of training into a structured approach that can be implemented in any therapeutic environment.

An approach is a way of looking at one or more problems, which helps the practitioner to understand both the causes and the effects of these problems, and different practitioners are influenced and subscribe to different approaches. An approach will also suggest ways of reducing and/or overcoming problems. For example, the developmental approach views problems as signs of delayed stages in normal human growth, and tackles problems by taking the client through a developmental sequence of learning. The neurodevelopmental approach, developed by Dr K. and Mrs B. Bobath, views problems related to cerebral palsy as signs of arrested motor development caused by interference with the normal maturation processes of the brain (i.e. through a brain lesion) and that immature reflex activity causes poor posture and movement patterns. This approach suggests that problems can be reduced or overcome by special handling techniques which help to stimulate and develop normal patterns of movement. Alternatively, the creative approach suggests using art, drama, music and movement to develop interaction and social skills, and to allow all clients the opportunity to express themselves in a variety of ways. This particular approach can be readily incorporated into other approaches.

We subscribe to the three approaches mentioned above, and to others, but have found the three that we have included in this book — i.e. the creative approach, normalisation and the behavioural approach — particularly useful because of their general adaptability and compatibility with other approaches. Normalisation helps in the creation of a therapeutic living and working environment, the behavioural approach provides a structured yet flexible teaching system and the creative approach enhances and broadens learning opportunities. References for these approaches are included in the chapters where they are discussed; the Further Reading list includes more specific and wide-ranging references about other approaches to training.

The aim of all work in this field is to increase the quality of life and independence of each client, and to help them to live fulfilling lives in their local community. To achieve these aims, clients need specific assessment, intensive training and opportunities to practise newly acquired skills. We have found, through experience, that training is more effective when each client's needs and progress can be related to an overall sequence of skill development. Our approach is to view independent living skills training as a sequence of three broad levels — basic, intermediate and advanced — each of which reflects stages in the normal development of independence. Each level is concerned with mastery of some type of independent living; basic skills involve acquiring functional independence, intermediate skills involve acquiring independence within a sheltered or assisted environment, and advanced skills involve acquiring the ability to live independently away from regular support. We have also found that, by placing training activities in the context of one of these levels, it is easier for the staff involved firstly to define training objectives, and secondly to maintain the therapeutic orientation of training sessions over a period of time. Additionally, by structuring similar activities into three timetabled levels, each client is able to draw on the right level of training for his or her individual needs. For instance, clients may need to draw on basic motor activities to meet their functional needs, but on intermediate activities for their cognitive and perceptual needs. By superimposing individual teaching sessions on top of selected timetabled activities, training can be tailored precisely to the client's needs.

This book is far from being a definitive text, but by selecting various approaches, techniques and methods of problem-solving that we have found useful, we hope that we have provided a starting point from which more and more experience can be accumulated. The information we have included is information we would have liked to have found in one book when we were new to the field of mental handicap, and we hope that it will be of use for anyone who wants to acquire a good basic understanding of a therapeutic approach to the provision of training opportunities and the meeting of clients' needs.

Christine Peck
Chia Swee Hong

1

Meeting Needs

Meeting the needs of clients is everyone's responsibility.

Working with people who have a mental handicap is not easy; it can often be stressful, difficult, unpleasant, dirty, and mentally and physically demanding. There may also be little immediate evidence of the effects of any training carried out, although in the long term real progress may be easily seen. Progress is usually the result of consistent training over a long period of time, and this takes not only adequate staff resources (in terms of hours of work) but also staff of the right calibre. To meet these training needs staff must be selected primarily because of their suitability for the work, rather than primarily because of their previous experience or qualifications (or both).

Professionally, trainers need to have a combination of the right attitudes, an understanding of relevant theory, experience in the technical aspects of their work, and effective interpersonal skills. The EDURP/NHSTA[1] research project, concerning advanced competency in therapists working in the field of mental handicap (1985–1986) defined these qualities much more precisely in their report (the Green Book). One of their conclusions was that the use of the term 'mentally handicapped' is not compatible with desirable attitudes. They felt that mental handicap (if it had to be referred to in those terms at all) should only be used as a clinical diagnosis or method of identifying special needs, and not as a way of referring to specific individuals.

Personally, a whole range of different attributes may be desirable. Mittler (1977)[2] suggests that some of the personal qualities required are self-confidence, stability, a sense of humour, optimism, an interest in people, patience, tolerance, adaptability, the ability to work with other team members and the capacity to be a good model. Hewitt (1966)[3] suggests that teachers of emotionally handicapped children need to have objectivity, flexibility, the ability to structure work, curriculum expertise and the skills for intellectual modelling. York-Moore (1976)[4] suggests that therapy in its broadest sense, in the management of children with Down's syndrome, requires:

(1) sincerity in the desire to help, and the willingness to give freely of one's time in order to listen to problems being aired;
(2) patience, even when an individual makes little or no progress, and the ability to give parents or other carers the support and encouragement they need;
(3) enthusiasm for each project;
(4) love, and the readiness to return affection in the form of a kiss or cuddle.

Meeting the needs of those who have a mental handicap, which is the subject of the rest of this book, is therefore something that requires people with very special qualities and abilities, irrespective of training, qualifications or status. Approaches and philosophies to training may vary, but all are reliant on suitable staffing levels to meet each individual's needs. However, staff also have needs which have to be met, e.g. continuing education and development, having their contribution to training valued or receiving support from colleagues, without which they may find it difficult to cope with the demands placed on them.

STAFF RESOURCES

People need to work in an environment which allows them sufficient time to carry out their work effectively. In helping clients to acquire independent living skills, much time has to be spent in carrying out individual training programmes; without this individual training, progress can slow down, and staff can become less able to assess their own value and performance. Ideally, staffing levels should provide enough time for every client's training objectives to be adequately met.

Table 1.1: National Development Group rating scale[5]

Group	Level of handicap	Ratio
I	Independent, no problems Needs minimal support	1 : 8
II	Semi-independent, needing some supervision Mild behaviour problems	1 : 6
III	Dependent with mild behaviour problems Needs training	1 : 4
IV	Multiple handicap, severe behaviour problems Needs care	1 : 1

Justifying the number of staff needed can be difficult. The National Development Group[5] used a rating scale (Table 1.1) which links nursing levels to the dependency of the clients. Although this scale was specifically aimed at nurses, it could usefully be applied to other staff groups. Once staffing levels have been calculated from these figures an extra 26 per cent then has to be added to cover annual leave, sickness and training. However, the National Development Group used this scale to establish staffing levels for long-term residential units, and smaller residential units or community homes probably require more staff. These figures should therefore be viewed as a minimum. Additionally, in *Helping Mentally Handicapped People in Hospital* (1978)[6] the National Development Group recommended that the following nursing ratios were the absolute minimum required when working with children:

One person to two profoundly or severely handicapped children
One person to three less severely handicapped children
At no time during the day should the staff : client ratio be less than 1 : 3

The National Development Group state that these figures are only put forward as recommendations. In the same report the National Development Group strongly recommend a considerable increase in the number of consultant psychiatrists, psychologists, occupational therapists, physiotherapists and speech therapists, but cannot identify the desired level of increase. Each of the professions mentioned above has its own professional association which recommends minimum or appropriate staffing levels.

3

Training and education

In-service training should be provided for everyone, to encourage them to acquire the desired levels of skill, and also to help them to take stock of the processes at work, the relative merits of different approaches and their role within a team. Any system of on-going education should include:

(1) *Basic theoretical concepts.* Any educational programme should be multidisciplinary, involving everyone irrespective of experience. Only those aspects that it is absolutely essential for everyone to know and use should be included, and teaching should include plenty of opportunities for informal practice.
(2) *Reviews of work.* Theoretical tuition needs to be backed up by appropriate practical experience, time to discuss and evaluate the issues involved, and time to develop professional confidence. Many aspects of work in this field raise moral and ethical questions which need to be openly discussed. Equally, reviewing work should include a staff appraisal system, which gives feedback on performance and time for all members of staff to identify their own needs and goals.
(3) *Visits.* Visiting other units is one of the best informal methods of education, demonstrating successes, failures, achievements and plans in other similar units. To be really useful, visits need to provide a broad experience of all the facilities available, and staff sent on visits should be encouraged to bring back and share as much information as possible.
(4) *Attending relevant courses.* Courses run by outside agencies can meet a variety of needs, e.g. education, development of skill, creating links with other groups of staff or broadening of knowledge. Attendance at courses also enables staff to introduce new ideas and developments into training, which ultimately provides a better service for the client group.

WORKING TOGETHER

Meeting the needs of clients, in a field which involves more professions than ever before, requires the use of a team approach. However, effective teamwork ultimately depends on the quality of the communication and liaison between many different people. When decision-making is shared (as in a team approach) traditional areas of responsibility become less clear; staff take on work on the basis of their ability to meet needs rather than in relation to their job title, and this can be very threatening. People can sometimes see the team approach as a way of sharing failure and losing credit for individual successes, although a well-established team can, through pooling ideas, expertise and mutual support, meet client needs more effectively.

The implementation of the team approach varies, and different people use different terms, e.g. multidisciplinary and inter-disciplinary. Basically all terms refer to a system where all those involved with one client meet regularly to evaluate, modify and plan a co-ordinated approach. Meeting together, though, is not an end in itself, and multidisciplinary teams must also be able to clearly outline decisions taken, and the reasons behind those decisions, and then disseminate that information to everyone concerned. This, in turn, obviously increases the demand for written summaries, record sheets and minutes. Most methods of work have occasional formal planning meetings or conferences for major evaluation, goal-setting and forward planning, and regular team meetings for monitoring performance, recording progress, or making changes to training programmes. The main difference between a conference and a team meeting is the breadth of representation; the time relationship between the two can vary considerably depending on the needs of each client.

The primary function of a formal planning conference is to review overall progress and take major decisions regarding future goals, objectives, placements, etc. This requires representation from every agency and profession involved with the client, including the client and his relatives, so that decisions can be made and common approaches to training can be adopted. The time and date of such meetings need to be circulated well in advance to allow each person time to prepare any relevant information he may have. Decisions and agreed objectives should be written down on a summary sheet and forwarded to the team meeting.

The team meeting decides how the goals set at the conference can be met. These meetings are usually attended by staff who work regularly with the client being discussed; the meetings draw on subjec-tive opinion as well as objective information for the planning of individual programmes. Minutes should be kept of each meeting, including details not only of action to be taken, but also of the reasons behind any decisions made. In some instances it may be useful to use summary sheets such as the example shown in Figure 1.1.

Figure 1.1: Individual training summary

Name   Date of team meeting
Address   Date of next review
Key worker   Date of last conference
Date of next conference
Current conference objectives
    a.
    b.
    c.
    d.

Review of Previous Goals

Goal	When achieved	Discussion & decisions taken

Current Training Goals Agreed by Team Meeting

Current goals	Action being taken	By whom	Signed

Other Discussion & Decisions Taken

Signed .... Date ....

It is important that decisions made at team meetings, by a majority vote if necessary, are carried out or implemented by everyone involved. This may mean that individual members of staff have to carry out programmes that they disagree with, at least until discussions can be re-opened at the next team meeting, but without accepting this aspect of teamwork, consistency and continuity of training are difficult to ensure. However, it is equally important that all team members understand (and are able to use) their right to attend the next meeting and renew discussion on decisions that they believe are wrong, dangerous or unworkable.

Working together as a team also requires individuals to know each other personally and professionally. However, when there is not always the time to get to know other team members, it is very easy to apply previous experience of professions (good or bad) to current colleagues and, in effect, prejudge their attitude, personality and contribution to the team. Human prejudice is natural and very difficult to remove, but being prepared to learn more about the skills different professions can offer, and relating to each member of staff on a personal as well as a professional level, can help to break down barriers and avoid duplication of workload.

Two groups of people often forgotten in the team approach are those who most need to be included — the clients and their relatives. These two groups of people should attend meetings whenever they want to, rather than having to wait for an invitation to a specific meeting or conference. Clients who either have difficulty in expressing their views, or who may appear not to understand the issues involved in discussions, need to have someone representing them at either type of meeting. Consequently, one of the most important roles within a team is that of key worker or co-ordinator. The role of a key worker or co-ordinator is:

(1) to ensure that clients have regular conferences and team meeting discussion;
(2) to check that conference decisions are forwarded to team meetings for discussion and that training programmes drawn up by the team are implemented;
(3) to formulate training programmes with relevant professionals and teach the administration of the programmes to other staff;
(4) to ensure that records are kept;
(5) to forward and contribute special knowledge about clients to each conference or team meeting;
(6) to provide a 'family' relationship, e.g. in purchasing clothing

7

and the creating a private living environment;
(7) to be an advocate if necessary.

Ideally each key worker or co-ordinator should be responsible for, or involved with, only one client.

SUMMARY

Multidisciplinary teamwork is an effective method of meeting everyone's needs in this particular field, as it makes best use of scarce staff resources and provides a better service to the client group. However, this approach needs better than usual standards of interpersonal and interprofessional communication. The Association of Professions for the Mentally Handicapped produces a booklet entitled *Working Together*, which highlights many different aspects of teamwork in a positive and useful way.[7] Ultimately meeting needs depends on achieving a balance between what is available and what is desirable, and on using different skills to best advantage.

References

1. EDURP, *Therapy in Mental Handicap — advanced competence* (a twelve-month research and development project for the Educational Development Unit for Remedial Professions, 1985–1986). EDURP is now part of the National Health Service Training Authority (NHSTA).

2. P. Mittler, *Day Services for Mentally Handicapped Adults* (National Development Group, Pamphlet no. 5, 1977).

3. F. Hewett, 'A Hierarchy of Competencies for Teachers of Emotionally Handicapped Children', *Exceptional Children*, vol. 33, no. 1 (1966), p. 712.

4. R. York-Moore, 'Physiotherapy Management of Down's Syndrome', *Physiotherapy*, vol. 62, no. 1 (1976), pp. 16–18.

5. *Development Team for the Mentally Handicapped, First Report 1976–1977* (HMSO, London, 1978).

6. National Development Group, Helping Mentally Handicapped People in Hospital (DHSS, London, 1978).

7. K.A. Humphreys, *Working Together* (Association of Professions for the Mentally Handicapped, London, 1979).

Further information

Allen, K.A. *et al. Early Intervention — a team approach* (University Park Press, Baltimore (1978))

2

Normalisation

Normalisation wants every client to experience normal family and community life.

The ideas of normalisation are best known through the work of W. Wolfsenberger,[1,2] and have developed from a greater awareness of the effects of institutional life. As more is understood about the consequences of removing people from their family and local community the ideas of normalisation have gained ground. Normalisation does not seek to make clients 'normal', but does want everyone to have experience of normal family and community life. The normalisation approach starts by looking at the rights of clients, and suggests that many problems can be solved by either making changes in the environment or by raising staff morale and expectations. This involves questioning existing procedures and practices, and may potentially be very threatening.

The rights of clients have been defined by many people, including the United Nations.[3] An APMH (Association of Professions for Mental Handicap) report,[4] entitled *Better Services — the Realities*, suggested that specific rights for clients who have a mental handicap are:

(1) access to patterns and conditions of life which are as normal as possible;
(2) a normal daily routine including vocational activity away from home;
(3) a normal yearly cycle, e.g. holidays;

(4) a normal life cycle;
(5) a friendly and familiar environment;
(6) self-determination;
(7) integration with community life;
(8) normal financial consideration, e.g. social security and other benefits.

Professor Joan Bicknell took this view a step further in the 1983 Elizabeth Casson Memorial Lecture,[5] when she outlined rights as the right to:

(1) life and the chance to live;
(2) childhood and a normal family environment;
(3) take risks, make choices and take the consequences of decisions;
(4) not overburden their families and be free from parental decision-making in adult life;
(5) leave home and live in ordinary housing;
(6) work and acquire leisure skills;
(7) friendships, privacy, personal achievement and sexuality;
(8) ordinary as well as special services;
(9) worship, baptism, confirmation, marriage and a decent burial;
(10) make contracts, sign hire purchase agreements, mortgages, to vote and to sign consent forms.

Undesirable responses to a client (which ultimately affect their rights) can begin either when a handicap is diagnosed at birth, or when performance falls behind expected norms. These responses lead to lower expectations being placed on the client; lower expectations lead to reduced opportunities; reduced opportunities lead to reduced experience; and reduced experience leads to reduced performance. This lower performance confirms original expectations, and so restricted access continues.

Normalisation aims to: (a) maintain access to normal rights and experiences by breaking this self-perpetuating sequence as early as possible, and (b) change attitudes that result in segregation, the provision of special facilities, and the infantilisation of clients who have a mental handicap. These are long-term aims, but normalisation principles can also be used to improve existing facilities, where many clients who have a mental handicap already live in non-family environments. In these situations normalisation effects changes in buildings, work/living/social groups, personal appearance, teaching methods, attitudes, the amount of choice and decision-making each person has access to, and public perceptions of handicap. It also requires anyone working in large residential units to challenge every working practice and procedure by asking questions such as:

Would I like to live here or do this?
How and where did I learn the skills that I am teaching to others?
Am I teaching skills that everyone learns, or am I teaching skills that make residential life easier?
Am I teaching skills in appropriate environments?
Does every activity have to be initiated by staff?

To apply normalisation principles to present resources, it is helpful to look at the environment, living and working groups, opportunities for choice and chance and age-appropriateness.

THE ENVIRONMENT

Most people expect their homes to be places where they are valued, and where they can relax, express themselves freely, and do what they want. However, although living in a home-like environment does a great deal to develop positive and appropriate skills, clients may also have to be taught *how* to live in and make use of their home. Residential units, including group homes and individual flats in the local community, need to be planned and developed with the people who are going to live in them, and provided with enough support staff to give clients the training they need to integrate into their local community.

Residential units may have rules and regulations to follow which, although designed to increase protection and safety, do little to enhance the development of a homely atmosphere. Older buildings may have little space for storing personal possessions, bedrooms may have to be shared and have little privacy, furniture may be chosen because of safety standards and bulk-ordering requirements and covered in PVC instead of fabric because of 'incontinence', and living areas may be large and unimaginatively decorated. All this creates an environment that most people would not accept within their own home, yet the majority of these problems can easily be solved, e.g. by having chairs with fabric loose covers, that can be washed when necessary. Consideration of the environment is therefore important because:

(1) there is little point in setting up training if the client has limited opportunities to use and practise these skills in his living environment;

(2) some behaviours are the result of restricted environments/resources/facilities, and it is wrong to implement training programmes to correct these behaviours when making changes to the original environments/resources/facilities would have the same effect;

(3) the development of new skills and behaviours should always occur in the context of the environment where they are to be practised.

The primary concern should be the protection of the client's privacy, and this means that staff must accept that they have no right to enter an individual's room without permission. To achieve this, some physical changes may have to be made, e.g. observation panels in bedroom doors removed or covered up.

After privacy, the next most important considerations are the facilities available and the domestic arrangements of the home. It is very difficult to create ordinary, domestic environments if the furniture, equipment and daily procedures undermine any efforts made. Lack of facilities, such as electric sockets, in bedrooms can stop clients from using electrical items (except those that can be run on batteries), so some building modifications may need to be considered. Similarly, while it is possible to do a great deal to disguise old and institutional furniture, often the only real solution is to dispose of it and buy newer, more appropriate items. Living rooms that are large and uninviting can be made more homely by the addition of rugs, plants, pictures and carefully thought out lighting — as long as lamps and rugs can pass safety regulations! The use of colour and different lighting levels can effect quite major changes without the need to alter the building structurally.

Daily routines can be the most handicapping of all environmental aspects. The lack of privacy and dignity that comes with communal bathing, washing and toileting facilities (especially where clients are physically dependent), shared clothing or large, shared bedrooms should never be accepted. Such practices de-personalise living environments for everyone, and if they still exist, should become priority areas for change. If clients cannot have dignity and privacy in the most personal aspects of daily life, then there is little point in altering the more general aspects of the environment such as colour, design and decor of buildings.

Some daily routines can handicap people in less obvious ways by removing opportunities for challenge and decision-making. Staff may be employed to do the domestic work, meals may arrive ready cooked or assumptions may be made about what each client wants to do, and each of these actions, although done for the benefit of the client group, can take away individual opportunities for self-determination and responsibility. In order to avoid this it is essential that the living environment should be organised as an active learning experience. The ideal environment is one which stimulates and reinforces desirable activities and behaviours, which encourages each individual to be as independent as possible, and which provides living experience which is as much like a family unit as possible.

LIVING/WORKING GROUPS

The larger a living group becomes, the more need there is to impose some organisational system on to it. How this is done depends on the physical structure of the living unit and the number of staff available. Poor environments are often characterised by:

(1) having a large number of rules, and very good reasons for not breaking them in individual cases;
(2) residents sharing resources, space, clothing and so on, with no chance of privacy even in the bathroom or toilet;
(3) staff (and residents) wearing uniforms, or the same types of clothes — in normal life a group of people with mixed interests and likes/dislikes have very different ideas about the sort of clothing they like to wear, but people living in residential units can often look very similar;
(4) very little individual contact with clients, during self-care procedures, meal-times, teaching sessions, outings, or leisure activities;
(5) set times for meals, getting up or going to bed, which cannot be changed because changes create difficulties for the staff;
(6) the use of surnames (and titles) by staff and residents, e.g. Sister Jones — this does nothing to break down hierarchical barriers and teach clients how to relate more appropriately to people; formal names and uniform often go hand in hand, and it is much more difficult to call someone 'Sister Jones' if she is not wearing a uniform;
(7) perceiving and identifying clients by their clinical characteristics

rather than by personal characteristics, e.g. 'the Down's syndrome girl' rather than 'Jane, the girl with long black hair';
(8) continually talking to clients in a loud voice, at a superficial level, or in an infantile manner.

Getting the best out of any staffing group is difficult because staffing levels always fluctuate. However, small family-sized units show the best overall results in terms of the quality of training provided, the appropriateness of the environment and the flexibility of approach.

MAKING CHOICES AND TAKING CHANCES

Growing up in a family means experiencing choice-making and chance/risk-taking in a wide variety of contexts. Choice can often be removed from clients because (a) relatives or carers feel that an individual is unable to make an appropriate decision, (b) choices about a group of people are usually made by the staff or carers, and (c) there is often no way for choices made to be implemented. Obviously any large organisation needs to have structure to its workings, but it also needs to allow clients to:

(1) use equipment without having to ask permission, e.g. switching on TV sets or radios;
(2) have access to a variety of options, including the option to do nothing;
(3) choose what happens to them routinely, e.g. when they eat meals or go to bed;
(4) be able to make choices when shopping, dressing, eating, etc.

Choice should also be timetabled into any work or training programme, where there should be either a choice of activity or a choice about whether or not to attend. The latter option is especially important on a work training programme, where clients have to learn about the reciprocal effect their choices have, e.g. on pay levels in relation to the amount of work completed.

Chance and risk are often removed from clients if they live in residential units. Access to dangerous equipment, materials and situations can be restricted without any consultation with the clients. Normalisation principles require that unreasonable levels of protection should be removed, and clients allowed to learn through the usual process of trial and error. This is reasonable up to a certain point, but as is the case with a growing child, certain risks can be allowed, while others are far too dangerous to be considered. For example, it is reasonable to allow small children to discover that water from a tap can sometimes be hot, but unreasonable to allow them to play with a kettle of boiling water. The same sort of protective risk-taking needs to be applied to clients. The deciding factors need to be age, ability and understanding in relation to the likely risk; if individuals are unable to understand, or protect themselves from, the risks involved then it is unreasonable to allow them to learn in this way.

Staff involved in allowing risk-taking firstly have the problem of deciding on the level of risk that is appropriate for each individual to take, and secondly, may have to live with the criticisms of senior staff, relatives and other carers if something goes wrong and a client is hurt. Obviously, team meetings can decide on the general level of risk-taking that is appropriate, but there will always be situations where an individual member of staff has to take decisions about the level of risk-taking permissible, and it is these situations that leave staff vulnerable. Risk-taking, therefore, needs to happen in a supportive working environment, and with the agreement of everyone concerned.

AGE-APPROPRIATENESS

Age-appropriateness is, as the term suggests, used to describe possessions and behaviours suitable for the age of each client. For example, a bottle of whisky would not be an age-appropriate present for a 2-year-old child, but would be for an adult, and words such as 'moo-cow' and 'baa-lamb' may be age-appropriate for a young child, but are not age-appropriate for adults. Age-inappropriateness can be a problem for adult clients, particularly those who have not grown up in a family environment where different age-related behaviours are easily seen.

Confusion can arise over the difference between the chronological and mental age of a client, e.g. if an adult has a 'mental age of 5 years', then to treat him as a child of 5 would be to deny him age-appropriate interaction. To be age-appropriate, the approach to clients needs to be adult, but tailored to their needs and ability levels. Clothing and appearance also need to be critically appraised to ensure that clients do not have attention unnecessarily drawn to them because of the inappropriateness of their appearance.

Home and living environments can easily become age-inappropriate, by containing childish books, posters and toys. For example, some adult clients lavish a lot of attention on dolls, which is obviously not age-appropriate, and to deny them access to dolls may seem hard, yet a pet may give them the same opportunities to demonstrate a caring and loving relationship, but be more age-appropriate. Training and leisure activities are also areas where problems can occur. Very often the equipment used for training may be developmentally appropriate but childish, because only equipment made specifically for children is available. This is especially true of educational equipment and books. Alternatively, activities may be age-appropriate but the actual content may be wrong. For example, a day trip to the coast may be age-appropriate for adults, but playing on the beach all day is not.

The best way of preventing age-inappropriate behaviour is to discourage it from developing. However, when inappropriate behaviours and habits have developed, altering them needs great tact and patience, because age-inappropriateness is usually related to very personal aspects of a client's life.

SUMMARY

Normalisation is not something that is provided for clients who have a mental handicap, but a system for designing and providing the life experiences necessary to fulfil each client's potential, both in daily life and in planning for the future. It requires constant thought and self-appraisal from those involved, e.g.:

(1) Do I offer opportunities for learning experience and challenge in the way I use the environment, community facilities, activities or interests?
(2) Does the work/training/experience I provide meet individual needs, and can it be quickly adapted to meet changing demands?
(3) Do I involve community resources as much as possible in the training I provide?
(4) Does my work increase the chance of normal community experience for each client?
(5) Is all planned training likely to be achieved?
(6) Do clients integrate well in terms of appearance, behaviour, competence and ability when they use community facilities?
(7) Is the training I offer age-appropriate, i.e. would other people of

the same age and experience be doing similar things?
(8) Can I find many examples of each client having opportunities for privacy, individuality, choice and chance?

If the list of questions above produces any 'no' answers, then the ideas of normalisation should be re-examined and appropriate changes made to the training and living environments.

References

1. W. Wolfsenberger, *Normalisation* (National Institute of Mental Retardation, Bethesda, Maryland, 1972).

2. W. Wolsenberger and L. Glenn, *Programme Analysis of Service Systems (PASS III)* (National Institute of Mental Retardation, Bethesda, Maryland, 1975).

3. United Nations, *Declaration of the Rights of Disabled Persons*, 1975.

4. D. Philip-Miles, *Better Services — the realities* (Association of Professions for the Mentally Handicapped, 1974).

5. J. Bicknell, 'Mentally Handicapped People: their rights and responsibilities', *British Journal of Occupational Therapy*, vol. 46, no. 6, (1983), pp. 157–60.

Further information

H. Brown with Jan Alcoe, 'Lifestyles' — a staff training pack based on normalisation principles (ESCATA, 6 Pavilion Parade, Brighton BN2 1RA, 1985). Packs also available for work in other specialties.

P. Rowan, *What Sort of Life?* (National Foundation for Educational Research, Windsor, 1980).

J. Ryan and F. Thomas, *The Politics of Mental Handicap* (Penguin, Harmondsworth, 1980).

A. Tyne, *The Principles of Normalisation — a foundation for effective services* (Campaign for Mentally Handicapped People, 1981); adapted from work by John O'Brien.

3

The Behavioural Approach

The behavioural approach uses reinforcement as the main agent of change.

The behavioural approach is based on the theory of operant learning (particularly as developed by B.F. Skinner and others), and is complex yet logical in application. Its use requires acceptance of the view that behaviours (good and bad) are learned, and that consequently behaviours can be changed by manipulating the learning process.

Operant learning is one of two main types of conditioned learning, the other being classical conditioning/learning. Classical conditioning occurs when an association is formed between a conditioned stimulus (i.e. one that has no previous connection with the response) and an existing behaviour (unconditioned response) which can already be elicited by another stimulus (unconditioned stimulus). By repeated association, the conditioned stimulus becomes linked with unconditioned response, and can produce a response that is very similar, if not identical, to the original unconditioned response; this new learned response is called a conditioned response. This process is clearly seen through Pavlov's experiments with dogs. Pavlov observed that dogs salivated at the sight and smell of food (unconditioned response) and by associating a bell (conditioned stimulus) with the delivery of food, he was able to produce salivation to the sound of the bell alone (conditioned response). Both the unconditioned and conditioned stimuli produced the same response.

Operant conditioning is similar in some ways to classical

19

conditioning, but it changes behaviours by reinforcing or rewarding desired behaviours *after* they have occurred. Classical conditioning elicits certain behaviours in *response* to a presented stimulus; operant conditioning does not require any stimulus to be present to produce the desired behaviour, but relies on the subsequent reinforcement/reward to teach new responses (e.g. a dog salivates in response to food, but does not usually beg for it). Skinner demonstrated operant learning with rats kept in a box which was completely empty apart from a lever with a food dish beneath it. In the process of wandering around the box, a rat would occasionally press the lever, causing a pellet of food to drop into the food tray. The lever-pressing behaviour was reinforced by the food and gradually the rat learned to press the lever specifically to get food.

In daily life the two types of learning occur concurrently, but in formal learning situations they are often separated. Operant learning is particularly useful in solving specific learning or behavioural problems, because change occurs through the positive manipulation of interaction and environment, and the behavioural approach makes full use of this as a teaching technique. The behavioural approach has two main principles:

(1) that the reaction/response to any behaviour determines the likelihood of that behaviour being repeated; and
(2) that a behaviour is defined as anything which can be seen/perceived, described and measured.

Behaviours can be divided into problem behaviours and skill-related behaviours. Problem behaviours usually refer to previously learned inappropriate behaviours, and skill-related behaviours usually refer to performance areas where the client needs to progress developmentally. So, examples of problem behaviours might be hitting, screaming, urinating in public, or running away, but would *not* be frustration, anger, annoyance or boredom. Problem behaviours associated with frustration, anger, annoyance and boredom can indeed occur, but only the physical manifestation of such feelings can be defined as 'behaviour' in this context. For example, boredom could only be measured subjectively, but screaming, head-banging or falling asleep (which may be symptomatic of boredom) can be seen/perceived, measured and described more objectively. Examples of skill-related behaviours are usually functional, e.g. visual tracking, manual dexterity, eating, drinking or dressing. The use of the word 'behaviour' in this chapter refers equally to both areas.

To make the most effective use of the behavioural approach it is essential that all aspects of its use are understood. This chapter looks at five main areas — the environment, the definition and observation of behaviour, reinforcement, intervention techniques, and the use of programmes and recording charts.

THE ENVIRONMENT

The environment in which intervention takes place is crucial to the success of this approach, and behaviours must always be considered in the context of the environments in which they occur. There is little point in using an intensive training programme for any client if the general environment in which he lives and works restricts opportunities to use and practise the skills being taught. Equally, it is also pointless to use a specific training approach if the same results might be obtained by re-organising or changing the environment. Many inappropriate behaviours first develop in response to inadequate environments and, while the behavioural approach can be very successful in reducing or eliminating inappropriate behaviours, the best approach (if possible) is to work towards preventing the initial development of inappropriate behaviours. The ideal environment is one which prompts and reinforces appropriate responses and behaviours, and offers varied opportunities for the client to engage in acceptable activities. The environment should also be stimulating, interesting, and actively encourage clients to initiate and explore. Achieving an ideal environment is made easier when living and working groups are small.

Specific teaching areas may need to be more structured, and allow staff to alter the arrangement of resources to meet differing needs. Generally, the more able the client, the more visual stimuli can be included in a teaching room, but a client whose concentration is poor initially benefits from being taught in small, functional rooms. When skills have developed in specific settings, the environment then needs to be changed to allow the client to tolerate progressively more stimulating environments, and ultimately cope with any situation.

21

OBSERVING BEHAVIOURS

Detailed observation of behaviour is most commonly found in relation to problem behaviours, whereas information about functional problems tends to be gathered by assessment. However, the principles of observation apply to both types of behaviours.

Once a behaviour has been identified as needing intervention, it needs to be precisely defined in order for information about its characteristics and frequency to be gathered. Exceptions to this may occur when general information about various behaviours is needed, and lead to observation charts where each member of staff uses his own words to describe a behaviour when it occurs. However, this gathering of general information is often followed up by a more specific record of an individual behaviour.

Behavioural definitions should be as detailed as possible in relation to the recording method chosen. At this point inter-rater reliability, or the accuracy with which different people interpret and apply the same description of a behaviour, should be checked. Generally, the more detailed the description, the better the inter-rater reliability is, but detail should always be balanced against brevity in order to make recording charts as effective as possible. The easiest method of checking inter-rater reliability is to ask several people to watch a video or observe a demonstrated behaviour, and then ask them to fill in a record chart using the initial definition of a behaviour. An agreement of more than 85 per cent is usually seen as satisfactory, but if there is less than 85 per cent agreement the definition of the behaviour to be observed needs to be more accurately described. For example, the definition 'verbally abusive' would probably lead to less than 85 per cent accuracy, whereas 'verbally abusive, i.e. swears, verbally threatens and/or shouts abuse for more than 10 seconds', is likely to get a higher level of inter-rater reliability.

Once the behaviour has been adequately defined, and inter-rater reliability established, the method of gathering the information must be decided. Usually the more discreetly the information is gathered, the more accurate it is likely to be; observations which require written recording are always obvious, but more discreet recording methods, e.g. using wrist counters, are available if recording can be based on numerical rather than descriptive information. There are various methods of gathering information, some of which are described below:

(1) *Continuous recording*. This involves recording *everything* a client does within a specific period of time, which in practice is very difficult to carry out. Videotaping can make this type of observation easier, but analysing the taped material is time-consuming. Nevertheless, continuous recording can be useful in establishing the frequency of a range of behaviours in certain clients, as long as staffing levels can be temporarily increased to either observe and record, or to analyse the videotapes. One disadvantage is that staff observing clients are very easy to spot by both clients and other staff, and this can result in 'staged' or 'provoked' incidents.

(2) *Event recording*. This involves recording every occurrence of a defined behaviour over a given period of time. This is useful in comparing initial frequency with frequency after a period of intervention, and can usually be managed within normal staffing levels because data can be collected numerically.

(3) *Duration recording*. Some types of behaviours are not separate events, but are continuous, e.g. crying. Duration recording measures when these behaviours occur and the length of time they last for.

(4) *Interval recording*. This is used to discover when behaviours occur within a given period. The period (e.g. 10 minutes) is divided into equal intervals (e.g. 1 minute), and the observer then records whether or not the designated behaviour occurs within that period, irrespective of the number of times it may have occurred. Again, this requires a high staff input and can be obvious to the clients who are being observed.

(5) *Time sampling*. In time sampling, regular times are chosen (e.g. every 15 minutes) and at those times the observer records whether or not the defined behaviour is occurring. The defined behaviour can have occurred between these times, but if it is not occurring at the chosen time it is not recorded. This method is economical of staff time, and can be useful in toilet training programmes, but may not always yield sufficiently detailed information.

After a suitable period of observation the data are analysed and used to help make decisions about management of the behaviour. Data are usually summarised in chart or diagram form, like the examples in Figures 3.1 and 3.2.

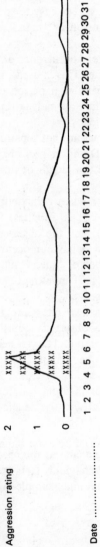

Figure 3.1:

Aggression rating

2

1

0

0 = No physical aggression
1 = Physically hurts self
2 = Physically hurts others
x = Menstruation

1 2 3 4 5 6 7 8 9 10 11 12 13 14 15 16 17 18 19 20 21 22 23 24 25 26 27 28 29 30 31

Date ....

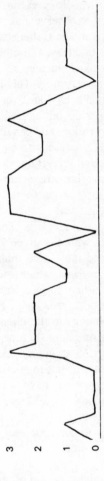

Figure 3.2

Number of tantrums per day

4

3

2

1

0

1 2 3 4 5 6 7 8 9 10 11 12 13 14 15 16 17 18 19 20 21 22 23 24 25 26 27 28 29 30 31

Date ....

A tantrum is any incident where X shouts, screams, hits others or himself, stamps feet or throws objects, for more than 30 consecutive seconds.

REINFORCEMENT

Reinforcement is the agent of change in the behavioural approach and can be either given to increase the frequency of a behaviour, or temporarily withheld or withdrawn to decrease the frequency of a behaviour. Giving reinforcement in response to desired behaviour is easily understood but the *withholding* of reinforcement must be carried out in an environment where, for the majority of the time, appropriate behaviours are demonstrated and programmes are structured to allow the client a reasonable chance of receiving reward. The withholding of reinforcement should make up less than 20 per cent of all interactions; if it makes up more than 20 per cent the client may see this procedure (i.e. producing inappropriate behaviours, waiting for the reinforcement to be withheld, producing the desired change, and then receiving reinforcement) as the normal way of achieving a desirable response.

Reinforcement need not always involve things which are generally seen as pleasant, enjoyable or purposeful. Unpleasant responses can often becoming reinforcing because of their association with something pleasurable. For example, if a client discovers he can get more attention by being naughty than he can by being good, then he may eventually (through association) find being told off (or even punished) desirable, and ultimately find this negative interaction reinforcing in itself. Many stereotyped responses can be traced back to inappropriate associations such as this.

Reinforcement can be divided into two types — positive and negative. Negative reinforcement is often confused with punishment, but it is important to remember that *both* types of reinforcement describe methods of giving something which is pleasurable, and punishment (except where it has been inappropriately associated with pleasure) is obviously not pleasurable. Positive reinforcement describes any interaction where something pleasurable is given in direct response to a desired behaviour. It is often the preferred method of reinforcement because:

(1) it makes the teaching environment and the teaching experience more pleasant and motivating;
(2) the rewarding response always happens after the action has been completed (whereas in negative reinforcement the rewarding response is given immediately the desired action begins);
(3) it stops the teaching session from becoming aversive;
(4) it is much easier to understand and use, which is an important

consideration when many people may participate in carrying out programmes.

Negative reinforcement also describes a situation where something pleasurable is given in response to a desired action, but the pleasurable response usually takes the form of escaping from, or stopping, something that is disliked. For example, the positive reinforcement for making eye contact could be a cuddle, or a drink, or something else liked by the client; in negative reinforcement the clients would have to work in the presence of something they disliked (e.g. loud noises), and make eye contact in order for the noise to be switched off. Another name for negative reinforcement is escape training, because it teaches clients to carry out certain actions in order to escape into a more preferred activity (Premack's Principle). Negative reinforcement provides much more control over the learning situation, but equally requires much more specific use.

Premack's Principle is often used automatically in training activities, because it involves a common-sense approach to motivation. Basically it says that people will carry out activities that are not particularly attractive to them in order to gain access to more pleasurable activities. So, a child who has to finish his homework (a less preferred activity) before watching television or meeting friends (a more preferred activity) will probably produce more work than a child who watches television or meets his friends before doing his homework.

In daily life, positive and negative reinforcement are often linked within a single interaction. For example, in a mother/child relationship the child may produce progressively worse behaviour in demanding something to eat. The mother may firmly resist giving the child anything up to a certain point, when she gives in. In this instance the child uses negative reinforcement to manipulate his mother towards the desired action, and the mother positively reinforces the child's behaviour. The result of this interplay is that the child learns how to get something to eat, and the mother learns how to avoid a situation she dislikes, and both will use this learning the next time the same situation occurs. If the situation arises regularly the child may learn to increase the level of the precipitating behaviour in order to reduce the amount of time the mother takes before she escapes from the situation (and gives food). In the training situation, joint use of positive and negative reinforcement needs to be carefully controlled.

Reinforcers are actual items, events or responses that are pleasurable and rewarding. Reinforcers can be classifed in various ways, but the most usual are shown below:

(1) *Primary reinforcers.* These are things which satisfy basic human needs, e.g. food and drink. They are the most immediately effective form of reinforcer because their value does not have to be taught, and because the giving of food and drink is a regular event. They are particularly useful for clients who have a small range of enjoyed activities or events. Physical contact can also be seen as a primary reinforcer.

(2) *Secondary reinforcers.* This type of reinforcer has no value in itself, and cannot satisfy basic needs, but the reinforcers acquire value through their association with more pleasurable items, i.e. they are conditioned reinforcers. For example, tokens or money gain value because they can either be used to purchase desired items, or lead to desired social interaction. This type of reinforcer can be very effective, although the value often has to be taught by pairing the secondary reinforcer with a primary reinforcer, followed by the fading out of the latter.

(3) *Social reinforcers.* These reinforcers require the highest conceptual ability because their value depends upon an understanding of abstract ideas and social values. Like secondary reinforcers, they are conditioned reinforcers. Verbal praise is the most common reinforcer, and is the one reinforcer that should be used alongside all others. The ultimate goal of using reinforcement is to teach a behaviour and then maintain it with the minimum support; verbal praise is the best medium for maintaining previously learned behaviours. Also, by pairing verbal praise with an existing reinforcer, verbal praise becomes a conditioned reinforcer. Other types of social reinforcer — e.g. status, salary, respect or compliments — rely on the client wishing to be seen positively by others.

Variety is essential when choosing reinforcers for training purposes, as repetitive use of one or two reinforcers can actually work against the training goals because of the boredom or satiation that is created. This is particularly true when using food and drink as reinforcers; size of reinforcer is also important. Primary reinforcers, i.e. food and drink, should have a marked texture and/or taste, and should be given in small quantities that can quickly be consumed. As a guide, pieces of food should be approximately the size of a raisin, and

27

drinks given at approximately 5 ml at a time. These amounts may be small, but if used repeatedly during a training session the amount of food or drink taken can mount up, and reinforcers should whet the appetite for more, not satiate it!

Secondary reinforcers should be measured in terms of number or access time. If the reinforcer is access to a preferred activity, then the reinforcer needs to be measured in time; if the reinforcer is money or tokens, then it is easy to numerically measure the reward. As social reinforcers reflect a client's desire to be part of a social group no firm guidelines can be given, except that the size of the reinforcer should avoid over-praising or under-praising expected levels of behaviour.

When selecting reinforcers, information can be gathered by talking to everyone who knows the client, by testing the client's reaction to various reinforcers, or by measuring the difference various reinforcers make to the performance of an existing skill. The administration of reinforcers needs to be done very carefully to avoid reinforcing the wrong behaviours. A reinforcer must therefore be given:

Clearly: i.e. its value/significance must be obvious to the client;

Immediately: i.e. it must occur directly after the desired behaviour;

Contingently: i.e. it must only be given for the complete desired behaviour;

Consistently: i.e. it must be given every time the desired behaviour occurs.

If reinforcers are administered poorly, other less desirable behaviours may be encouraged. For example, if a client is reinforced correctly every time a Makaton sign is copied, signing skills are likely to develop, but if between demonstrating the sign and receiving reinforcement the client screams, then screaming will be reinforced, and probably increase in frequency.

Initially, reinforcement should be given each time the desired behaviour occurs, but once learning has taken place this level of reinforcement should be reduced. Stopping all reinforcement immediately is not effective, as the original behaviour reappears relatively quickly (this is more usual with problem behaviours than with skill-related behaviours). The frequency of reinforcement is gradually reduced/faded out; initially this might mean reinforcing every other occurrence of the defined behaviour, then every third occurrence, and so on, and would eventually lead to a random frequency of reinforcement. By making the frequency of the maintenance reinforcement variable the client is unsure of when reinforcement will be forthcoming, and as long as a reasonable level of reinforcement is maintained, the client will continue to be motivated by the *possibility* of a reward. If a combination of reinforcers is used, the primary and/or secondary reinforcers should be faded out completely before making verbal praise random.

Reinforcement, then, is a central part of the behavioural approach, and understanding the principles of reinforcement is crucial for success. Problems frequently arise from misunderstanding what is required, and it is equally important to know the difficulties as well as the advantages of using reinforcement. Common problems associated with the use of reinforcement are:

(1) misunderstanding of the two types of reinforcement, e.g. using punishment but calling it negative reinforcement;
(2) using inappropriate and poorly chosen reinforcers;
(3) using too much or too little of each reinforcer;
(4) administering the reinforcers poorly;
(5) giving reinforcers too infrequently;
(6) fading out reinforcers too quickly;
(7) keeping reinforcement at a high level and not fading it out.

INTERVENTION TECHNIQUES — SKILL-BUILDING

In the behavioural approach, specific techniques are often necessary to teach new skills. Generally, most skill-building techniques use positive reinforcement, while many of the intervention techniques use negative reinforcement. Very few of the techniques described below are used individually, and most can be carried out either within formal teaching programmes, or as part of an informal management approach.

Modelling

Modelling teaches new behaviours by prompting the client to copy, and is therefore also called imitation. The person modelling the new skills needs to be someone as much like the client as possible, or someone who is particularly liked or respected by the client. Ideally

the model should demonstrate the desired behaviour while another person leads the teaching and prompts the client, but if this is not possible, then good results can be obtained by positively reinforcing other clients who model desired behaviours in front of the person being taught.

Clients must be able to perceive the modelled behaviour accurately, and be able to achieve or reproduce it. This means that the client must be able to concentrate for appropriate periods of time, and be able to imitate. Individuals who find it hard to imitate may initially respond better to a combination of modelling and shaping.

In specific programmes the client sits or stands opposite or next to the model. The model demonstrates part or all of the task, and asks the client to copy the action; if the client can independently copy the action, reinforcement is given straightaway, but if the client needs help, the desired action is prompted before reinforcement is given. General use of modelling is based on the assumption that clients will copy the behaviours of people they work with. This means that staff need to be conscious of the importance of modelling desirable attributes in appearance, attitude to work, attitude to others, manners and interactions. It also implies that modelling should be a continual, but informal, training process.

Prompting

Prompting is a frequently used technique, and one which is common in daily life. It encourages clients to perform actions by using various levels of support and encouragement. There are three types of prompts:

(1) *Physical prompts.* This is physical guidance given in varying degrees to help the client complete an action. Physical prompts may be used, for example, to help encourage spoon-feeding or any other functional activity, and can vary from a full physical prompt to a very slight touch. Physical prompts are even more effective when used in combination with verbal and/or gestural prompts.

(2) *Gestural prompts.* This type of prompt uses gesture to indicate a course of action. A gestural prompt should mimic the movement required, e.g. pointing to a ball and then pointing to the person it should be given to, and to be really effective they should be used together with verbal prompts.

(3) *Verbal prompts.* A verbal prompt is simply a reminder to do something that includes relevant information, yet remains concise and succinct. Verbal prompts are often identical to key phrases used in teaching programmes, e.g. 'Give the ball to Tom', and they should always be paired with gestural and/or physical prompts.

Prompting as a single technique is most successful in teaching simple skills with only one or two component parts. However, it can be used in combination with other teaching techniques to encourage a wide variety of skills. Once a new behaviour has been established, the amount of prompting given should be reduced in a process known as fading. However, prompts need to be faded out carefully; if faded too quickly the client may miss the regular reinforcement and fail to complete the task, but if faded out too slowly the client could become over-dependent on the reinforcers used. Practically, the last part of any prompt should be faded first.

There are two methods of fading physical prompts. Firstly, support can be reduced throughout the whole task (while maintaining constant physical contact), by moving the point of prompt further away from the original position. For example, in a spoon-feeding programme, initially a full hand prompt may be used, but as the client progresses, the position of this prompt may change to a half hand prompt, then move to the wrist and then the forearm, before finally fading out completely. The second type of fading out involves maintaining the same prompt position throughout the task, but breaking the physical contact at certain points. Using spoon-feeding again as an example, the whole task would be prompted by a full hand prompt, but the prompt would gradually be removed for parts of the process. Initially this might mean removing the prompt during the downward (gravity-assisted) movement from mouth to bowl, and then replacing it once the spoon was in the bowl; gradually more of the task would be completed with the prompt removed, until eventually the client could carry out the whole task. The choice between the two types of fading depends on the client and on the task. Gestural prompts are usually faded by reducing the size and quality of the gestures, while verbal prompts are usually only reduced in frequency.

Shaping

Shaping is also known as 'successive approximations' because change occurs by reinforcing behaviours which progressively develop into more accurate versions of the target behaviour. To use shaping, a target behaviour must be linked to an existing behaviour which faintly resembles it. The existing behaviour is then slightly, often imperceptibly, changed and reinforced until completely accepted by the client. Successive changes move the existing behaviour nearer and nearer to the target behaviour, until the target has been achieved. Shaping is highly successful in areas where staffing levels are low, or resistance to other techniques may arise, and is equally useful with both skill-related and problem behaviours. A good example of its use with skill-related behaviours is changing existing spoon-feeding skills into cup-handling skills, by gradually making the spoon more and more like a cup. It is particularly useful in dealing with problem behaviours where confrontation between staff and client is undesirable. The difference can be illustrated in the example of a client who refuses to sit within a group of people, and consistently remains at the edge of the room. An intervention technique would require staff to confront this problem and take obvious action, whereas shaping would accept the present position of the client and gradually move the client's chair nearer to the group (or vice-versa). If the change in position is sufficiently gradual, the client should eventually end up sitting happily within the group.

Obviously, shaping is a technique which requires more time to achieve its end results than others, but this can often be advantageous, and provided each step is graded appropriately, shaping also reduces the risk of failure.

Chaining

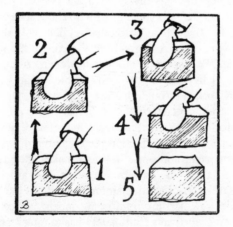

Chaining is a very powerful teaching technique because it allows complex skills to be broken down into component parts, and constantly reinforces previously learned elements. Prompting is also an essential element in any chaining programme. To use chaining, the target task first has to be broken down into its component parts with the size, range and difficulty of each part varying according to the needs of the client. After this stage, two methods of teaching are available — forward and backward chaining.

Forward chaining takes the component parts of the task and begins by teaching the first stage. Once the first stage has been learned, the second stage is introduced and is practised along with the first stage; the same procedure happens with each subsequent component until the whole task has been taught. Backward chaining takes the same task, and teaches the last stage first. Once this part has been learned, the previous stage is introduced and practised with the learned component; this process is repeated until the whole task has been taught. So, in a four-part task where 1 is the first stage and 4 is the last stage, the difference in teaching order between the two types of chaining could be expressed as:

Forward =   1 . . . 1+2 . . . 1+2+3 . . . 1+2+3+4
Backward =   4 . . . 3+4 . . . 2+3+4 . . . 1+2+3+4

Both types of chaining can be effective, but the differences between them make each of them suitable for teaching different skills. In both types of chaining reinforcement occurs at the end of the task, but in forward chaining there is always a point between the previously learned stage and the new stage at which reinforcement is currently being given. In effect, this means that a client will always reach a point where further work is required to achieve the same level of reinforcement. Backward chaining, however, places the newly introduced stage in front of previously learned stage(s), so that once the client has worked through the new component, the remainder of the task is instantly recognisable as the start of a procedure which leads to reinforcement. Reinforcement is therefore always given at the same point (i.e. on completion of the activity), which not only underlines important concepts, but also makes the giving of reinforcement easier (giving reinforcement in forward chaining can fragment the task). Backward chaining also allows the client to take over from the trainer, thus reinforcing independence, whereas in forward chaining, the trainer ultimately has to intervene and prompt new skills, which can emphasise dependence. Backward chaining is consequently often the method of first choice.

INTERVENTION TECHNIQUES — BEHAVIOUR MANAGEMENT

The best way to reduce problem behaviours is to eliminate the conditions that encourage them. All intervention techniques assume that problem behaviours have developed because they have been inappropriately or inadvertently reinforced, and these techniques therefore describe methods of ensuring that access to whatever is reinforcing a behaviour is strictly controlled. Many techniques assume that attention is the reinforcing agent, and withhold that attention until appropriate behaviours are demonstrated. With any technique of this kind, withdrawing or withholding attention inevitably makes the frequency of the behaviour increase, as the client repeatedly tries to gain attention through previously successful methods. If intervention techniques are successfully used, problems may worsen for a few weeks, after which there should be a noticeable reduction in the level of the problem. If, however, the intervention programme is stopped during the period of worsening behaviour, then there is a real possibility that the client will maintain the worsened level of behaviour permanently. This is an important factor to consider when using intervention techniques because *all* staff must be willing and able to cope with the temporary increase in problem behaviour until improvement occurs.

Extinction

Extinction assumes that the reinforcing agent is attention, and that changes can be made by controlling access to attention. This means that attention is withheld for inappropriate or undesirable behaviours, and attention is given for appropriate or desirable behaviours. Withholding attention basically means ignoring every behaviour that is being produced — i.e. nothing is heard, seen, perceived or felt, and no personal reactions are shown. This makes extinction a technique which requires practice and self-control. However, if applied appropriately it is an extremely useful technique for reinforcing the acceptability of different types of behaviour.

In practice there are several problems that staff using extinction should be conscious of. Firstly, extinction has to be used whenever the target behaviour occurs, and by every person coming into contact with the client. Extinction will never work where some people implement a programme and others either are unaware of the correct procedure, or unwilling to follow it. This is especially important where visitors are concerned. Secondly, the frequency or severity of a problem behaviour often increases dramatically after implementing an extinction programme, as the client tries to gain the attention that is being withheld. Thirdly, extinction can be very slow in achieving noticeable results, or even appear to actually worsen a problem, and thus lead to management programmes being abandoned prematurely. Finally, extinction can be dangerous to use with some types of problem, e.g. self-abusive behaviour, and is virtually impossible to use if there are many reinforcers for a single problem behaviour.

Reinforcement of incompatible behaviours

This technique uses an existing behaviour to reduce the frequency of another less desirable one, through the incompatibility of each behaviour. This is usually most useful with stereotyped behaviours, as incompatibility needs to be based on the impossibility of physically performing two actions concurrently. For example, if self-slapping is the undesirable behaviour, and it never occurs when the client is playing with jigsaws, then jigsaw play should be actively reinforced. The idea is that by reinforcing a range of positive behaviours and appropriate interactions, the stereotyped behaviour will decrease in frequency and eventually disappear. However, in some instances it may be necessary to temporarily reinforce incompatible behaviours that are not appropriate but nevertheless more desirable than the target behaviour; this is known as differential reinforcement.

Differential reinforcement

This is a composite technique combining extinction and reinforcement of incompatible behaviours, and can be useful with clients who have few obvious reinforcers, but a number of problem/stereotyped behaviours. In principle, all inappropriate or undesirable behaviours are identified and placed in order of priority (i.e. the worst or most difficult is first), and available reinforcers are also identified. The first target behaviour is then totally ignored, while every other behaviour (good or bad) is reinforced until the target behaviour disappears. The next most urgent target behaviour is then chosen, and the process repeated, until all problems have been dealt with. A crucial aspect of this technique is the introduction and reinforcement of a sufficient number of positive skills/interactions, in order to allow the client to eventually acquire more appropriate behaviours. Also, constant reinforcement of all behaviours can pressurise the client, and the aim should be a balance between reinforcement and over-reinforcement.

Time out from reward

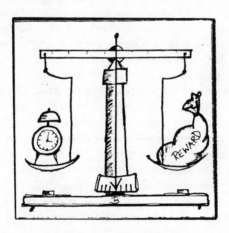

This technique is usually referred to as 'time out', although its full name is 'time out from reward', and it is a specific form of extinction. It is an intervention technique where clients are removed from circumstances that they find rewarding (to a non-reinforcing environment) for a specific period of time, and then brought back to the original situation, where they hopefully will continue to interact/work appropriately. The removal and reinstatement of the client from and to a given environment should be carried out in a neutral fashion, following the rules of extinction, and should occur immediately after a problem behaviour occurs, and not when time is available. Once the client has returned to the original situation, interaction resumes as usual; if the client is praised on return to the original environment it is possible that this will be seen as desirable in itself, and be actively sought by the client. Similarly, any evidence of time out being viewed as a game should make staff query the suitability of this approach.

The control of reinforcement may occur either through removing the client from a certain situation, e.g. to a separate room, or removing the reinforcing circumstances from the client, e.g. food. If clients are being moved, the new area should be as uninteresting as possible, and certainly not be a room such as a bedroom. Removing reinforcement may involve simply physically turning away from a client or actively removing something; in the latter instance it must be possible for this to be easily removed.

However, this technique is only successful when applied to people who value access to the circumstances they are removed from; it is pointless using time out with someone who wants to avoid work/interaction/activity, as removal will only reinforce effective methods of avoiding certain circumstances. Once it is clear that a client values the circumstances which are to be withheld, then the length of time that the client is removed from reinforcement is crucial. Experiments have shown that the most effective time out period is less than 3 or 4 minutes. The actual length of time varies according to the needs and abilities of each client, but the period must be long enough to emphasise the difference between a reinforcing and non-reinforcing situation, yet short enough to ensure that the client connects the intervention with the inappropriate behaviour(s). The client's concentration span is a useful indicator of the appropriate length of a time out period. If time out lasts too long it becomes seclusion, and clients will dissociate the intervention from their behaviour, find alternative things to do, or produce further undesirable behaviours through boredom or frustration.

Practically, there may be problems in administering this technique. Firstly, the problem behaviour may not have disappeared by the end of the initial time out period. If this is the case, contact must still be made at the end of the period, but it should be as neutral as possible, i.e. entering the time out area, and leaving without any interaction or response if the behaviour is still present. This avoids the possibility of time out developing into seclusion, maintains links with the original reinforcing situation and emphasises that readmission to a given situation is contingent on the elimination of certain behaviour(s). Alternatively, the client may be able to return to the original situation after the first period of time out, but then reproduces the same problem. In this instance the time out procedure should be repeated as if it were the first occurrence of the procedure.

Occasionally, problems arise in actually moving a client into a time out area. If this is likely to happen, first consider alternative methods of time out, e.g. removing reinforcing circumstances from the client. If this is impossible, and removal from the situation is the best solution, then care must be taken to protect both the client and the staff carrying out the time out programme. The basic rules are (a) never attempt to move someone who is bigger/stronger than yourself and get help if you are in any doubt, and (b) use your bodyweight as advantageously as possible. The most likely problem is that the client will either pull away from you, or sit down on the floor; if this happens then the ensuing attempts to move the client into the time out area cancel out any hope of maintaining a neutral interaction. The easiest way to move a client safely and effectively is described below:

(1) Stand behind the client and take hold of his left forearm with your right hand, just below the elbow; at the same time take hold of his left wrist with your left hand.
(2) Place your right shoulder in the centre of the client's back, at 90 degrees to his body, while maintaining your hold on the wrist and forearm (you should need to bend your knees to do this).
(3) Maintaining this position, push forwards and upwards, using the momentum your weight gives you to propel the client in the direction you want.

Given that the way in which you apply your weight prevents the client from sitting down as easily, the unexpectedness of this approach then allows you to easily and safely move a client into the time out area. For stronger, more difficult clients, two staff can adopt the same approach, by one person reversing the instructions above, and both working together to move a client; it is virtually impossible to resist being moved by two people in this way. Practice is the key to using this handling method effectively; all advantage is lost if you cannot automatically implement it when required. Similarly, time out is often a misunderstood intervention technique, and should only be used in specific circumstances, and in conjunction with people experienced in its use.

Restraint

Used as a specific intervention technique, restraint requires the use of negative reinforcement, in that the client has to produce acceptable/appropriate behaviours in order to escape from a disliked situation, i.e. being held. The escape from restraint acts as the positive reinforcer. Physical restraint can also be an effective way of diffusing potential or actual violence, as well as a method of reducing the actual frequency of a problem. It is usually used in response to behaviours which arise out of a client's frustrations or anxieties, and which endanger the safety of other people. It should not be used in response to attention-seeking behaviours.

In containing potential problems, close restraint makes the client feel more secure and reduces the chance of others being injured; used as a intervention technique, physical closeness reinforces the restrictive nature of the response. For these reasons it is easier (if possible) to restrain someone when he is sitting down, using the method shown below:

(1) stand behind the chair and, leaning forward, cross your arms in front of the client;
(2) while doing this, take hold of the client's wrists (your left hand on his right wrist and vice-versa), then gently rest your elbows on the client's shoulders;
(3) maintain this position, using your body weight to restrain the client, until the problem behaviour subsides — in this position, whichever way the client moves, the restrainer is in control.

This is obviously impossible to carry out in certain instances, e.g. if the client is standing. The easiest way to restrain a standing client is to use the same principles, but stand behind and hold the client as securely as possible. Alternatively, use the method of moving a client given in the section on time out, but keep the client's arms close to his body. Keeping to the rear of a client is an advantage in any form of restraint, both to avoid unnecessary injury and to gain most effective control.

Restitution

Restitution requires the client to make good any disruption or damage that he causes, e.g. picking up any objects thrown and putting them back in their original place. It is another application of extinction techniques, and the basic rules of controlling responses and interacting in a neutral manner described in 'extinction' and 'time out from reward' should be followed. Restitution is best used with clients who dislike the extra work involved in making reparation for their behaviour; it is not a suitable technique to use with those who find the extra activity/contact rewarding. The client must also be able to connect the behaviour (the cause) with the response (the effect); if clients are unable to perceive this connection, then the technique teaches nothing and becomes punishing.

Practically, this technique will only work well if clients can be readily prompted into performing the actions required to restore the environment to its original state; if time and effort are needed to achieve this, then restitution may not be an effective technique to use.

Over-correction

Over-correction is a more extensive application of restitution, in that instead of just restoring the environment to its original state the client has to restore the environment to a greatly improved state.

41

Practically this is very difficult to implement, and depends greatly on the task involved. For example, if over-correction was used in response to a client throwing bricks, then theoretically the client should pick up more bricks than were originally thrown. This means that either the environment has to be deliberately prepared by leaving other bricks on the floor (not a good model if restitution/over-correction is going to be used), or each time the client picks up a brick it has to be put back on the floor until a sufficient number of bricks have been picked up. However, over-correction is effective in reinforcing skills where the client already knows what to do but needs to improve the standard of performance. For example, if a client is able to make his bed every day, but only pulls up the top covers without straightening the sheets beneath, then over-correction would require the client to strip the bed and totally remake it.

Like restitution, over-correction is not successful with clients who cannot connect their behaviour with the reasons for using this specific form of response, and unless carefully monitored to ensure that the response remains in proportion to the original behaviour, then over-correction can become punishing.

Punishment

Punishment is not a desirable intervention technique, but there are instances where controlled use of punishment may be effective.

Punishment (i.e. giving something which is seen as unpleasant or undesirable) is most effective when carried out in response to an easily identifiable behaviour which occurs regularly; punishment also needs to be quick and easy to administer. In normal life, children learn the meaning of the word 'no' through its association with unpleasant consequences, and this is probably the commonest reason for using punishment as an intervention technique.

There are, however, many problems in using punishment. Firstly, punishment (especially physical punishment) is extremely difficult to measure and quantify. Even when punishment is clearly defined in a management programme — e.g. a short, sharp slap across the back of the hand, or loss of access time to a desired activity — different people can apply punishment in many different ways. For example, a short, sharp slap can vary from a minor tap to a painful thump depending on the strength and understanding of various people. Secondly, the use of punishment can escalate as the client becomes used to a set level of response. This can be particularly worrying if physical punishment is used, or may lead to deprivation if punishment takes the form of restricting access to events and activities. Thirdly, punishment rarely stops a problem behaviour from occurring but usually teaches clients to take more care about the circumstances in which they demonstrate behaviours which lead to punishment. This can make life more unpleasant for the people within a client's living and work environments.

Generally, punishment is most effective as either a temporary or short-term intervention technique, or with clients who understand concepts of right and wrong behaviour and the consequences that certain behaviours bring. Many people actively disagree with the use of punishment and prefer to implement either a token scheme (described in the next section) or a goal-planning approach. Both systems link rewards for desirable behaviours with the forfeiting of privileges for undesirable behaviours, and teach clients to take the responsibility for controlling their own problem behaviours.

USING TECHNIQUES IN PROGRAMMES

The success of the behavioural approach lies in the consistency of its use by everyone involved. Terminology and techniques need to be understood to avoid confusion, and clear and relevant records need to be kept. The behavioural approach can be rejected as having failed to work when in fact its principles have been misunderstood and misapplied. The commonest problems are:

(1) using a technique incorrectly;
(2) using, but not understanding the reasons behind, a technique;
(3) misunderstanding of the components of each technique, e.g. referring to the time out but in fact meaning seclusion;
(4) inappropriate use of techniques;
(5) inadequate teaching programmes;
(6) fear or reservations about using techniques.

Many people think that the behavioural approach can only be used to change problem behaviours, but do not also see its application as a method of teaching new skills. In fact the behavioural approach is used more frequently to teach new skills than it is used to reduce problem behaviours. The process of writing up both types of programme is described in more detail in Chapter 5. In actual use, single techniques are rarely used; composite approaches are much more common, but obviously need more care in application. Token programmes are good examples of a composite approach, where desirable behaviours are reinforced, undesirable behaviours are discouraged (through loss of earned reinforcers), and the ultimate reward depends on the balance between the two.

Tokens

A token can be anything (a plastic disc, metal rings or stars on a card) that has acquired value because of its association with a reward, e.g. it can be exchanged for something that is valued. This makes tokens conditioned reinforcers. Anything can be used as a token, as long as it is only available to the client through the token programme.

In a token programme the behaviours for which a client will receive and forfeit tokens are defined and explained to the client. At the same time the client chooses a number of desirable options, e.g. buying sweets, going to the pub or having access to certain activities or people, and a value expressed in numbers of tokens is attached to each option. The client then controls the number of tokens available for purchasing these options at the end of set periods, by deciding whether or not to perform the target behaviours. Meeting all the target behaviours allows the client to choose one (or more) of the options available. Losing tokens for undesirable behaviour restricts the choice of options available, and may prevent the client from being able to purchase anything.

Token programmes follow the same principles as any other behavioural programme, e.g. in the administration of reinforcers or defining target behaviours. In addition it is also necessary to:

(1) make the value attached to each chosen option reasonable and achievable;
(2) make the number of tokens earned/lost for each behaviour reasonable;
(3) decide the length of time between exchange points, e.g. spending tokens daily, twice-weekly or weekly — on established programmes a variety of expensive options, e.g. a weekend away, can encourage saving;
(4) decide where, when and how tokens are going to be given and exchanged;
(5) decide where, when and how tokens are to be forfeited.

Successful use of token programmes depends on accuracy, consistency and motivation. Some clients, however, will need to be taught the value of tokens before such a programme can be implemented. It may be necessary to teach clients not only how to exchange the token, but also how to look after it, and how to assess their running total. This is easier when clients have some understanding of number and saving, but for less able clients, charts with photographs or pictures of available reinforcers may be needed. Clients who need to learn the value of tokens should be able to exchange each token immediately after it has been earned. Obviously this limits reinforcing options to those that can be immediately available, but as the client learns that tokens can be exchanged for valued alternatives, then the concept of needing more than one token to gain access to reward can be introduced. Gradually, the value of each item can be increased to represent its true value in relation to the cost of performing each of the target behaviours. Initially, the choice of options for exchange can be less daunting if limited, but as the client progresses more choices should be included, so that decision-making can be encouraged, i.e. whether to spend all tokens on one option, or buy a variety of cheaper options. Equally, as the client becomes more adept in following the programme the exchange point can be varied from immediately, to hourly, to twice-daily, etc.

The ultimate aim of any programme is to maintain all new skills and appropriate behaviours with as little support as possible. Tokens are no exception, in that they are a very useful way of building up a range of behaviours, but should not be seen as a permanent training medium. Tokens, like any other form of reinforcement, should be faded out when the client has achieved the targets set. The main methods of fading out tokens are:

(1) pairing tokens with verbal praise, and then reducing the ratio of tokens : praise;
(2) increasing the exchange value of the options, i.e. either making the client do more for each token, or increasing the number of tokens required for each purchase option;
(3) ensuring that the environment will continue to reinforce appropriate behaviours without the need for tokens, e.g. paid work;
(4) increasing the time between exchange points;
(5) increasing the time between target behaviour and token giving.

Generally, token programmes are effective because of the constant emphasis on the links between appropriate and inappropriate behaviours. Tokens are also easier to use than other primary and secondary reinforcers, they allow the client to vary their reinforcers in line with current preferences and they avoid satiation, especially when primary reinforcers are being used. Administratively they are more flexible in use than other types of reinforcer, can help in the development of saving and shopping skills, and can help in building up a time delay between performance and reinforcement.

KEEPING RECORDS

Records need to be kept to chart progress and assess the degree of change that has occurred in relation to the use of any intervention technique. Record sheets should provide brief but informative details about the administration of any programme. More information about recording charts is given in Chapter 5.

SUMMARY

The behavioural approach is an effective tool that can help in improving each client's abilities to the full, and a flexible yet structured teaching system that can be used concurrently with various other approaches. It encourages positive interaction, improves teaching skills and provides ways of dealing with problem behaviours. It is also the basis of other approaches to training, e.g. goal-planning. Like the behavioural approach, goal-planning emphasises positive interaction, but goal-planning is more likely to solve problems through a client's strengths, whereas the behavioural approach works directly through a client's needs. Successful use of the behavioural approach requires a thorough understanding of the principles involved, but once these are understood the approach can be used flexibly to meet a variety of needs.

Further information

I. Illot, 'Goal Planning with the Severely Mentally Handicapped', *British Journal of Occupational Therapy*, vol. 44, no. 5 (1981), pp. 163–6.

E.A. Perkins *et al. Helping the Retarded — a systematic behavioural approach* (British Institute of Mental Handicap, Kidderminster, 1983).

W. Yule and J. Carr (eds), *Behaviour Modification for People with Mental Handicaps*, 2nd edn (Croom Helm, London, London, 1987).

4

Assessment

Assessment is the means through which objective information can be gathered.

Any assessment, from informal evaluation of information to specific testing and diagnosis, aims to gather objective data which will help in the making of appropriate decisions concerning training, needs and future goals. There are six main reasons for assessment:

(1) *For screening purposes.* Screening tests decide which people, in a large group, need specific training. They are usually applied to a group sharing some common characteristics such as age, sex, or geographical location, and they identify people within that group whose performance falls below expected levels (without giving reasons for the results). The routine sight and hearing tests carried out in schools are screening tests.

(2) *To identify current level of function.* Assessments of this type also compare the client to accepted levels of performance in a group of similar age, physique, culture, profession and/or intellectual ability. Unlike screening assessments, however, these tests are just as useful in identifying those people who exceed expected levels as they are in identifying low performance. There are many assessments of this type available, often related to different areas of function, such as the Coloured Progressive Matrices Set, and the AAMD Adaptive Behaviour Scale.

(3) *As a diagnostic tool.* Diagnostic assessments are usually norm-

referenced and can be used in conjunction with functional or criterion-referenced assessments in order to identify the reasons behind any problems or deviations from the norm. For example, if a client is making slow progress in reading, a diagnostic test such as the Marianne Frostig Developmental Test of Visual Perception could show that the client's difficulties were due to poor figure/ground discrimination. This sort of information provides a base on which to plan training.

(4) *To determine potential for training.* Conversely, some assessments may be carried out to confirm that there is no major obstacle that will prevent improvement in a specific area. No assessment can predict future levels of achievement, but particularly in developmental and functional assessments it is possible to determine that a client is ready and able to progress to the next stage of training.

(5) *To establish a baseline for training.* Assessments which can be regularly repeated are very useful in providing basic information against which to measure future achievements and progress. Baseline details must relate to the assessments used to monitor progress, and consequently the most effective assessments to use are those which provide both baseline and progress data.

(6) *To record progress and monitor change.* Particularly in long-term training, where progress is often slow and difficult to observe on a day-to-day basis, assessments which can demonstrate change are very useful. Ideally the assessments used should also be capable of recording baseline information, and should be brief enough to make regular re-assessment possible, yet detailed enough to provide accurate data.

To be useful and effective, any type of assessment has to take into account certain basic requirements, i.e.:

(1) The assessment should be appropriate to the needs and abilities of the client, and if at all possible, carried out by a familiar person.

(2) The assessor should be objective and unbiased in their approach to the client.

(3) The assessor should understand the difference between norm-referenced and criterion-referenced assessments. Norm-referenced assessments compare the client's performance to the known scores of other similar people, and so only include items which can demonstrate levels of ability or the achievement of

age-related skills. Criterion-referenced assessments compare the client to selected standards or levels of performance, and are more concerned with whether or not these performance levels are achieved than whether developmental norms are reached.

(4) All environmental and personal influences on the assessment procedure should be considered. The assessor should understand the effect that extraneous noise, the surroundings, the size of room, the type of equipment, etc. can have on the client, as well as attending to the client's personal needs, (e.g. toileting before assessment), or disabilities. The assessor should also be sensitive to the client's mood and to the degree and type of explanation needed.

LEVELS OF ASSESSMENT

Assessment can be carried out on three levels — informally, and using criterion-referenced assessments or norm-referenced assessments. Each type of assessment gathers a different type of information, and all three combine together to provide a complete picture of the client. In practice, criterion-referenced and norm-referenced assessments complement each other very well, and norm-referenced assessments tend to be used to monitor overall progress at certain intervals, while criterion-referenced assessments are used more frequently to check on the speed and quality of learning.

Informal assessment

Informal assessment is the way in which information about a new client is rapidly gained, or a means of monitoring on-going performance. It should involve all members of the training team as well as immediate family, relatives and friends. Informal assessment is often the main way in which changes or differences in performance are identified and referred for further investigation.

Criterion-referenced assessments

These assessments, which are often professionally published, aim to gather information about a client's abilities without comparing the results to the performance of a sample group. Generally, this means that criterion-referenced assessments provide a broader range of data than norm-referenced assessments, and both types can therefore work together to provide information that is as detailed as possible.

Criterion-referenced assessments often take the form of check-lists related to stages of development or areas of function, but there is no particular guide as to how frequently these assessments should be carried out. Frequency of assessment is decided by the needs of each client.

Norm-referenced assessments

These are assessments which enable decisions to be made on the basis of comparing one client's results with those obtained from other similar people. These comparisons to the sample group (known as norm-referencing) are researched and validated, and the assessments consequently include specific instructions for their administration. Very few norm-referenced assessments are unrestricted in use; some are only able to be administered by a psychologist. Norm-referenced assessments have recognised procedures which cover the administration, explanation, timing and scoring of the assessment, and they should be reliable (i.e. produc-ing the same results for different assessors), valid (i.e. measuring what they claim to measure), and accurate (i.e. results correlate well with other similar assessments). Although they help to confirm or reject previous observations/conclusions, and often indicate the direction that training should take, they also take time to administer, and some of the assessments can be expensive to buy. Additionally, because they tend to measure achievement in very specific terms, they are not carried out very frequently.

CHOOSING THE RIGHT ASSESSMENT

The choice of any assessment depends on the assessor having a clear idea of the depth, range and type of information required, and a working knowledge of the range of tests and assessments available. In practice, it is better to be skilled in the use of a few particular assessments than to have a little knowledge about many.

The following section outlines a *selected* range of assessments which can be used by those involved in training; some of the assessments look at general function, while others look at more specific skills. The assessments have been divided into groups related to their usage, i.e. general ability, physical ability, hand function, perception, communication, play and interaction, self-care, social independence, cognition/literacy/numeracy, independent living, work and leisure. Tests grouped together in one area may well have more general applications, and this classification is not meant to imply otherwise.

(a) General ability

Assessment: AAMD Adaptive Behaviour Scale.
Author(s): K. Nihira, R. Foster, M. Shellhaas and H. Leland.
Publishers: American Association for Mental Deficiency, 5201 Wisconsin Avenue NW, Washington DC, 20016. Available in UK from NFER-Nelson Publishing Company, Darville House, 2 Oxford Road, East Windsor, Berks SL4 1DF.

The scale is divided into two parts. Part 1 deals with adaptive behaviours and is organised along developmental lines, covering skills important to personal independence, i.e. eating, self-care, money handling or use of leisure time. Part 2 deals with maladaptive behaviour related to personality or behavioural disorders. In addition to the assessment, the booklet also contains a scoring sheet and a profile summary score. Scores are compared to a similar sample group.

Assessment: Behaviour Assessment Battery.
Author(s): C. Kiernan and M. Jones.
Publishers: NFER Nelson (worldwide).

The BAB provides a broad spectrum of assessment procedures which can be used in order to identify the individual's strengths and weaknesses, and lead to effective remediation. Each section consists of a set of items aimed at various criterion behaviours — reinforcement, inspection, tracking, visuomotor, auditory, postural control, exploratory play, constructive play, search strategies, perceptual problem-solving, communication, self-help skills and social skills.

Assessment: The Next Step on the Ladder Developmental Assessment Scale.
Author(s): G.B. Simon.
Publishers: British Institute of Mental Handicap, Wolverhampton Road, Kidderminster, Worcestershire DY10 3PP.

This assessment, which is designed for people with multiple handicaps, consists of six major skill sections — use of sight and hearing, movement, manual dexterity, social development, self-help skills and communication. It is also part of a book which sets out clearly the basic essentials for helping children with multiple handicaps to become more independent.

Assessment: Vulpe Assessment Battery.
Author(s): S. Vulpe.
Publishers: National Institute on Mental Retardation, 4700 Keele Street, Downsview, Toronto, Ontario, Canada.

The Vulpe Assessment Battery describes the developmental assessment procedure of a typical child between the ages of 0 and 6 years, including tests of competence in various developmental areas such as gross/fine motor activity, language, cognitive and self-help skills. It also includes a sequential teaching approach relating to the assessment process, programme and goal-planning, and teaching techniques.

(b) Physical ability

Assessment: The Paths to Mobility Checklist.
Author(s): J.L. Presland.
Publishers: British Institute of Mental Handicap.

Fourteen skills areas ranging from lying supine to using a wheelchair are given in this checklist. It offers the opportunity for noting down the criteria for success, the date first tested and the date first mastered, plus the results of a follow-up assessment for each individual. This book outlines methods for teaching very early posture and management skills to children.

Assessment: Reflex Testing Methods for Evaluating CNS Development.
Author(s): M.R. Fiorentino.
Publishers: Charles C. Thomas Publishers, 2600 Southfirst St, PO Box 4709, Springfield, Illinois 62708-4709, USA.

This handbook shows how reflex testing is done, by describing how to apply the appropriate stimulus and observe the responses, in order to see if reflex development is age-appropriate.

(c) Hand function

Assessment: Erhardt Developmental Prehension Assessment.
Author(s): R.P. Erhardt.
Publishers: Ramsco, P.O. Box N, Laurel, Maryland 20707, USA.
This test provides a detailed assessment of a range of motor skills and functions that contribute to the development of prehension. Three major sections measure skills from involuntary arm/hand patterns to grasp and release, and drawing skills.

(d) Perception

Assessment: Frostig Developmental Test of Visual Perception.
Author(s): Marianne Frostig *et al.*
Publishers: Consulting Psychologists Press Inc., 577 College Avenue, Palo Alto, California 94306. Available in the UK from NFER-Nelson.
The Frostig test assesses five areas of visual perception — eye–motor co-ordination, figure–ground discrimination, consistency of shape, position in space and spatial relationships. It provides information on the relationship of visuo-perceptual abilities to problems in school learning/adjustment, brain damage and other handicaps. The child's overall performance can be compared with the expected level of perceptual development for pupils of the same age.

Assessment: The Purdue Perceptual Motor Survey.
Author(s): Dr E.G. Roach *et al.*
Publishers: Charles E. Merrill Publishing Co. Ltd., Alperton House, Bridgewater Road, Wembley, Middlesex HAD 1EG (in the UK) and 936 Eastwind Drive, Westerville, Ohio 43081 (in the USA).
This is a widely used survey that identifies those children whose lack of certain perceptual motor abilities hinders their performance at school. There are 22 scorable items measuring various aspects of laterality, directionality and perceptual motor matching skills. The accompanying manual includes complete administration and scoring instructions.

(e) Communication

Assessment: The Wessex Revised Portage Language Checklist.
Author(s): M. White and K. East.
Publishers: NFER-Nelson (worldwide).
This checklist reproduces and expands the original language section of the Portage checklist. The skills assessed include the ability to listen, attend, imitate and play, the use of expressive language from early vocalisations, and the use of grammatical structures. The checklist, with its activity cards, acts as a guide to the design of teaching activities for the individual child.

Assessment: The British Picture Vocabulary Scale.
Author(s): L.M. Dunn *et al.*
Publishers: NFER-Nelson.
As no oral or written response is required for this test, it is suitable for use with a wide variety of people. It measures an important aspect of verbal ability — receptive (hearing) vocabulary. The results give a good indication of whether a child is of above average ability, or in need of special help.

(f) Play and interaction

Assessment: Parental Involvement Project (PIP) Developmental Charts.
Author(s): M. Jeffree and R. McConkey.
Publishers: Hodder and Stoughton Educational, Mill Road, Dunton Green, Sevenoaks, Kent.
These charts outline the skills which children usually develop during the first 5 years of life. The skills are grouped into five areas of development, i.e. physical, social, eye–hand, play and language. Each section consists of skills which lead up to the target items.

(g) Self-care

Assessment: The Mossford Assessment Chart for the Physically Handicapped.
Author(s): J. Whitehouse.
Publishers: NFER-Nelson.
This chart is a checklist of daily living skills, relevant to children

with mild to severe degrees of physical handicap. It covers: mobility, dressing, manipulative skills, personal hygiene, health, communication, reading, writing, mathematics, financial skills, domestic skills, and leisure activities. The results of the assessment are presented in the form of a pie chart showing skills which are being learned as well as those already mastered.

Assessment: Feeding Checklist.
Author(s): J. Warner.
Publishers: Winslow Press, 9 London Lane, London E8 3PR.
This checklist helps to identify problems in feeding and drinking. The accompanying manual, *Helping the Handicapped Child with Early Feeding*, gives some practical ideas and suggestions for handling the problems, e.g. finding suitable feeding positions and selecting feeding utensils, together with techniques for developing lip and tongue control and encouraging feeding/drinking.

(h) Social independence

Assessment: The Star Profile.
Author(s): C. Williams.
Publishers: British Institute of Mental Handicap.
The Profile is designed as a criterion-based record of social skills competence. Sixteen skills areas are covered including personal hygiene, physical function, educational ability, communication and social competence. The Profile follows four procedures: assessment, programme planning, implementation and evaluation.

(i) Cognitive, literacy and numeracy skills

Assessments: Boehm Test of Basic Concepts.
Author(s): Dr A.E. Boehm.
Publishers: NFER-Nelson.
This is designed to assess children's understanding of concepts considered necessary for achievement during the first few years at school. It enables the identification of, for example, children whose level of concept mastery is low, or particular concepts that are not understood by a particular child.

Assessment: Coloured Progressive Matrices Sets (A, Ab and B) and the Crichton Vocabulary Scales.
Author(s): John C. Rowen.
Publishers: NFER-Nelson.

The Coloured Progressive Matrices are suitable for people with a variety of disabilities, and are used to assess intellectual abilities up to the stage when a person acquires the ability to reason by analogy. The problems presented are relatively free from verbal instructions and are printed on coloured backgrounds to add interest. The Crichton Vocabulary Scales provide a complementary vocabulary test.

Assessment: Neale Analysis of Reading Ability.
Author(s): N.B. Neale.
Publishers: NFER-Nelson.

This widely used test consists of six graded oral reading passages which have been standardised for different ages. There are three parallel forms of the test — A, B and C — and three supplementary diagnostic tests are also included in the booklet. The results give scores for reading rate, accuracy and comprehension.

(j) Independent living

Assessment: Pathways to Independence.
Author(s): D. Jeffree and S. Cheseldine.
Publishers: Hodder and Stoughton.

These checklists look at eleven areas of skill which contribute to personal and social independence, i.e. eating and drinking, information, time, money, freedom of movement, use of amenities and leisure. Each booklet contains a profile sheet which provides a useful and immediate overall view of the client's abilities over a period of time, as an indication of his progress.

Assessment: The Scale for Assessing Coping Skills.
Author(s): E. Whelan and B. Speake.
Publishers: Copewell Publications, 29 Worcester Road, Alkrington, Middleton, Manchester M24 1PA.

This scale covers 36 areas of knowledge and skill which are central to independent functioning in the community. The profile of the individual facilitates the setting of realistic goals and a better use of resources.

Assessment: The Hampshire Assessment Materials (HALO and HANC).

Author(s): M.J. Shackleton-Bailey, B.E. Pidcock and Hampshire Social Services.

Publishers: Hampshire Social Services, Trafalgar House, The Castle, Winchester, Hampshire SO23 8UQ.

The Hampshire Assessment Materials were devised in 1981–2 in order to achieve standardisation of services for clients within the county of Hampshire. The assessment materials consist of:

HANC 2 Used by training centre staff and the handicapped person.

HALO (Hampshire Assessment for Living with Others). Used by residential staff and the handicapped person.

HANC F An interview schedule used with families/relatives and the client.

HANC S A school-based assessment for young people moving from school to training centre/social education centre/other placement.

Each client has only two assessments carried out — one relating to day placement (i.e. HANC 2 or HANC S) and one relating to residential placement (i.e. HANC F or HALO). All the assessments include sections on self-care, domestic skills, community living skills, communication, personality and social adjustment, close personal relationships, use of leisure, health/physical disability, group membership and employment. The assessment makes client participation an integral part of the process.

There is also a scoring sheet at the end of each subject area, and a training section which highlights the difficulty or ease with which improvements can be made for whatever reason, e.g. lack of resources, or lack of initiative.

(k) Work skills

Assessment: The Work Skills Rating Scale.

Author(s): E. Whelan and H. Schlesinger.

Publishers: Copewell Publications.

This scale has been designed to cover the important areas of skill required to be a successful worker. The resulting profile can help staff to identify areas where training or counselling may be needed, or to match the individual's current workstyle to the demands of appropriate forms of work.

(l) Leisure skills

Assessment: Junior Interest Profile.
Author(s): D. Jeffree and S. Cheseldine.
Publishers: The Winslow Press, 9 London Lane, London E8 3PR.
The Junior Interest Profile contains pictures of 16 activities. It aims to obtain two types of information from young persons: (a) their knowledge of, and participation in, various leisure activities; and (b) type of activity they would like to participate in, given the opportunity.

SUMMARY

Assessment is the only valid base from which training can be planned, allowing decisions to be made on the premise 'I know . . .' rather than 'I think . . .'. The various tools and media available for assessment change and expand rapidly, and staff involved in assessment of clients should attend study days and courses to keep their knowledge as up to date as possible. A range of assessment media should be readily available, to help staff compare and contrast the relative merits of various assessments.

However, irrespective of the experience and knowledge of the staff, assessment is only worthwhile if it leads to action, and forms part of the on-going process of meeting a client's needs. At its worst it can be a rigid regime of information collection; at its best it can be a tool that enables the right responses/interventions to be matched to each client's needs.

Further information

I.L. Coley, *Paediatric Assessment of Self-care Activities* (C.V. Mosby Co., St Louis, Missouri, 1978).
J. Hogg and N. Raynes (eds), *Assessment in Mental Handicap* (Croom Helm, London/Brookline Books, Cambridge, Massachusetts, 1987).
P. Mittler, *The Psychological Assessment of Mental and Physical Handicaps* (Methuen, London and New York, 1974).
H. Schofield, *Assessment Testing: an introduction* (Unwin International, London and Boston, 1978).

5

Individual Teaching Programmes

Teaching charts should be clear, concise and easy to use.

At some point it is necessary to draw together the different approaches, assessment data, teaching techniques and client needs into a co-ordinated plan. There are many different treatment planning systems, e.g. the Portage Project, that can provide a structure for programme planning, and be used in conjunction with a variety of approaches. The best system is the one which provides the best service for the client group. However, all treatment systems, irrespective of their individual differences, include:

(1) personal details;
(2) long-term targets/goals;
(3) short-term targets/goals;
(4) details of how the targets/goals may be reached, and the criteria for measuring success;
(5) details of specific and general needs related to all aspects of treatment.

Planning systems should relate closely to assessment data, and take into account (particularly with clients who will always need a high level of help and care) both the requirements for future placements, and the feelings/needs of the client, their relatives and care staff. Plans can vary a great deal, from those which are concerned with only one or two major problems, to those which deal with a variety of complex, inter-related skills and behaviours. It is often easier to write a training plan for a very profoundly handicapped client than it is to write one for a much more able client, who is learning to live independently in the community. This is usually because profoundly handicapped clients have clearly identifiable disabilities or developmental delays, whereas more able clients are learning the subtleties of applying a wide variety of skills in social, work and community settings.

Progress can often be slow and changes difficult to discern, so training plans help to show the general direction of training, and the goals that have been achieved so far. Training plans also help to maintain continuity through staff changes, i.e. clearly defined objectives and methods of work can be understood and carried out by new members of staff, even though they have not been involved in the original discussions and decision-making.

All training systems that define targets, goals and general trends need some way in which objectives can be translated into an active teaching tool. Individual teaching programmes are required for this, irrespective of the training system or approach adopted.

An individual teaching programme is simply a formalised method of writing down the details of a training programme. The behavioural approach subscribes to a very specific method of writing teaching programmes, which once mastered can be adapted to meet both formal and informal training demands. This method of writing a specific programme is described below, together with information about how the process can be adapted to produce a less formal programme. The behavioural type of teaching programme is equally suitable for the teaching of new skills and for the management of problem behaviours. However, the teaching programme is not an end in itself; teaching cannot take place in a vacuum, but must be carried out as part of a caring, working relationship. Teaching programmes must balance their formal, consistent, and precise approach with the need to interest, involve and motivate the client. The writing of a teaching programme has 4 main processes:

(1) information gathering,
(2) analysis of the task/behaviour,
(3) setting objectives,
(4) writing and evaluating teaching programmes.

INFORMATION GATHERING

As in the behavioural approach, information about the level of function, or type of behaviour, needs to be gathered to provide a baseline for training programmes, which must be able to show the level or frequency of a skill/behaviour *before* any action is taken. The information is gathered from those most closely associated with the client, and should include details of any obvious causes of problems and any action taken. Such information needs to be gathered over a period of time, particularly where problem behaviours are concerned, and 2 weeks should be seen as the absolute minimum observation time.

The accuracy of the information recorded is obviously crucial, and every effort should be made to remove undue bias, influence or misleading description from the recording chart. The charts in Figures 5.1, 5.2 and 5.3 are examples of how information can be collected. The type of chart shown in Figure 5.1 is the least reliable because it involves a variety of people describing and evaluating behaviours. However, it yields a lot of information about the behaviours and the reactions they cause, and can consequently be useful in identifying the variety of behaviours present, and in assessing the consistency or objectivity of the recorders.

Figure 5.1

Name: Record of:				Week beginning:	
Date	Time	Description of behaviour	Preceding behaviour	Action taken	Name

Figure 5.2

Name: Record of:	Mon	Tues	Wed	Thurs	Fri	Sat	Sun
Throws food on floor							
Spits food out of mouth							
Plays in food with fingers							
Refuses to eat							
Tips food off plate							
Steals food from others							
Eats inappropriately							
Demands different food							

Name: — Week beginning:

Figure 5.3

NAME: ACTIVITY: Completing six-piece inset board puzzle

+ = unprompted
x = completed with verbal and physical prompts
0 = refused to do puzzle

Date	Puzzles 1 2 3 4 5 6	Comments	Signed
15.5.86	0 0 0 x 0 0	Would not look or concentrate	CRP
16.5.86	0 0 0 0 0 x	As yesterday	CSH
17.5.86	0 0 0 0 0 0	Very upset — cried frequently	BU
18.5.86	0 0 x 0 x 0	Anxious — uninterested in puzzles	VB
19.5.86	0 x 0 0 x 0	Performance and interest variable	BU
20.5.86	x 0 x x 0 x	Alert and interested	CRP
21.5.86	x x x x x x	Much more interested in puzzles	SO

The chart shown in Figure 5.2 already lists the problem behaviours (fuller descriptions accompanying the chart may be necessary), and the observer has to tick the behaviours which occurred within a given period. This is likely to yield more accurate information, because it only requires the observer to make decisions about whether or not any of the listed behaviours occurred. An example of a completed chart is shown in Figure 5.3; this chart shows a client's performance in completing a six-piece inset board puzzle.

ANALYSIS OF THE TASK/BEHAVIOUR

Each skill or behaviour has to be broken down into its component parts so that its teaching can be accurately planned. However, before analysing any task, the following factors should be considered:

(1) the client's style of, and capacity for, learning;
(2) the speed at which the client is capable of assimilating new information;
(3) the complexity of the task;
(4) prerequisite skills that are necessary;
(5) the level of motivation that is necessary for success.

Consideration of these factors will help to decide on the depth and range of each analysis, and so avoid unnecessary work, but generally it is better to produce an analysis that is too detailed rather than one which is too brief. The analysis should finally consist of small stages or actions, each of which can be learned either separately or in conjunction with other parts of the same task. The following example (Figure 5.4) gives a brief analysis of what is required to complete the simple six-piece inset puzzle (see completed baseline chart in Figure 5.3 for this activity):

Figure 5.4

(1) Sit at a table, with the inset board directly in front of you and the puzzle pieces face upwards on the table on your dominant hand side.
(2) With your dominant hand, pick up a puzzle piece.
(3) Compare the piece in your hand with the vacant spaces on the inset board, and select the vacant space which correctly matches the puzzle piece in your hand.
(4) Steadying the puzzle board with your non-dominant hand, move the puzzle piece until it is 2–3 inches above the same-sized space on the inset board.
(5) Move the puzzle piece downwards towards the board until it lies on top of its matching space.
(6) Rotate the puzzle piece until, by keeping it positioned centrally over the space and pressing downwards slightly, the piece drops into the space.
(7) Repeat steps 1–6 with the other pieces on the table, until the puzzle is complete.

SETTING OBJECTIVES

Setting objectives helps to avoid any confusion about *why* teaching programmes are taking place. An objective is a description of the level of skill, or type of behaviour, that a client will have after a successful course of training. Objectives do not have to specify *how* these changes will occur; they only state the distance between two levels of performance. They can be long-term, i.e. describing what the client should be able to do in a year or more, or short-term, i.e. describing what the client should be able to do in less than 1 year. Some objectives can be seen as maintenance, i.e. keeping skills or behaviours at their current level for as long as possible.

Objectives are often confused with aims, but there are important differences between the two. Aims are general statements of the direction of training, e.g. 'to extend self-help skills to full independence so that Ann can be transferred to a hostel'. However, even aims should have some substance to them and avoid such vague phrases as 'to increase independence'! Objectives are much more specific than aims, stating in clear terms the precise level of performance to be achieved, e.g. 'Ann will, whenever appropriate, wash and dry herself, dress correctly in clean, pressed and colour coordinated clothes and check her overall appearance in a mirror, without any help or prompting'. Long- and short-term objectives are sometimes called terminal and teaching objectives, respectively. The example above is a long-term or terminal objective; a short-term or teaching objective arising from this might be 'Ann will wash and dry herself each morning, without help or prompting, before dressing with assistance'.

Written objectives should be relevant to each client's needs, be realistic and achievable, and be written clearly. Each objective should include the following information:

(a) the name of the client;
(b) what the client is expected to do;
(c) when and how the client is expected to perform the action described in (b);
(d) the level of performance necessary to indicate mastery of the action.

The two objectives below show how to put these points into practice.

John (a) . . . will hop on one foot (b) . . . while his hand is held (c) . . . and hop for 10 feet or more (d).

Sally (a) . . . will drink from a cup (b) . . . which she is holding with both hands (c) . . . without spilling anything (d).

In a formal chart the teaching objectives may be split under two headings — teaching objectives and criteria for success. This displays information more clearly, giving the description of the desired action under 'teaching objective' and the measurement of the level of success under 'criterion for success'.

WRITING TEACHING PROGRAMMES

An activity chart is a document which summarises training needs, and describes current teaching programmes. Activity charts are also called teaching charts, teaching programmes, behavioural programmes, and management programmes. An activity chart should contain all relevant information, yet be brief, readable and instructive. It should be written in a positive manner, and avoid any possibility of misinterpretation, or subjectivity. Examples of activity charts are given below in Figures 5.5, 5.6 and 5.7; the first activity chart shows how a very precise chart would be written from the task analysis given earlier in this chapter, while the others show much more informal methods of writing programmes. The numbers immediately to the left of Activity Chart 1 (Figure 5.5) refer to the explanatory notes on pages 66 and 68–71.

(1) Information

This section should contain everything needed to identify the client, and give basic details of the teaching programme. This seems obvious, but when a client is following several programmes concurrently, identification needs to be clear and easily accessible. It is also important to record details of when decisions are made and programmes started, so that staff who were not present can refer back to the relevant team meeting minutes.

(2) Aims

The aims should explain why the programme is being used, and show how the programme relates to long-term goals — in this case this programme will initially increase Mary's ability to manipulate and use objects, which in turn will enable her to become more

Figure 5.5: Example Activity Chart 1

NAME: Mary   TEAM AGREEMENT: 23.6.86
1. ADDRESS: CHART COMMENCED: 30.6.86
ACTIVITY: COMPLETING SIX-PIECE INSET PUZZLES
2. AIM: To develop Mary's hand–eye co-ordination and fine motor skills, so that she will be able to participate in play activities, and eventually apply these manipulation and co-ordination skills to functional activities such as eating and dressing.
3. TERMINAL OBJECTIVE: Mary will complete a six-piece inset puzzle correctly, without any prompting.
4. TEACHING OBJECTIVE: Mary will rotate and fit one piece from each puzzle into its hole, without any prompting (step (6) of the analysis in Figure 5.4).
5. TECHNIQUES USED: Backward chaining and prompting.
6. FREQUENCY: Six puzzles per session, one session per day.
7. CRITERION FOR SUCCESS: Five out of six puzzles completed correctly with no help for five consecutive sessions.
8. REINFORCEMENT: Positive reinforcement, verbal praise reinforcers.
9. EQUIPMENT: Six simple six-piece inset puzzles which have different sizes of the same shape, e.g. rectangles or triangles. Don't choose puzzles that have no right or wrong orientation, e.g. squares or circles.
10. PROCEDURE:
    (a) Sit Mary at a table with the puzzles nearby.
    (b) Choose one puzzle and take one piece out of that puzzle.
    (c) Put the inset board in front of Mary.
    (d) Take the puzzle piece you have removed and position it on the inset board so that it lies halfway across its hole, but is orientated wrongly.
    (e) Say 'Mary, finish the puzzle'. If she correctly fits the piece into the hole without further help, praise her, mark a + on the chart, and move on to the next puzzle, repeating steps (a)–(e).
    (f) If Mary does not respond, or fails to completely push the puzzle piece into the hole, take her right hand, say 'Look, like this', and help her to complete the puzzle correctly. Reinforce her as described above, mark a x on the chart, and move on to the next puzzle, repeating steps (a)–(e), but choosing a different sized puzzle piece each time (if relevant).
    (g) Repeat this procedure until all six puzzles have been completed.
11. INFORMATION: For more information, advice or help in using this programme, see either Mary's co-ordinator (Anne Potts), or Swee, Chris or John.
12. RECORDING CHART:

+ = unprompted   X = prompted

Date	Puzzles						Score	Comments	Signed
	1	2	3	4	5	6			

independent in her personal care.

(3) Terminal objective

This should describe the level of ability that the client will have if all stages of teaching are successful — in this case Mary is expected to be able to discriminate, make decisions and then manipulate puzzle pieces correctly.

(4) Teaching objective

This should describe the skill (which in this case is part of the overall task) currently being taught. In most cases each level of the task analysis will become the teaching objective for successive teaching programmes.

(5) Techniques used

It is not always essential to identify the teaching techniques used, but it can be useful to do so, to underline the differences between techniques. In the example, backward chaining has been chosen, but prompting is also involved to ensure a high success and achievement response.

(6) Frequency

This refers to the regularity with which the programme has to be carried out. In the example Mary has to complete the procedure six times during one session (using six different puzzles), and has to have one session per day. The word 'trial' can appear in this context, with frequency being described as 'six trials per session, one session per day'; 'trial' simply refers to each time that the teaching procedure is used.

The frequency decided upon will depend on the client's tolerance of intensive teaching, the ability to retain information, the urgency with which the client has to acquire the skill and the number of staff available. It may also be related to specific times, e.g. a feeding programme may have its frequency determined by mealtimes. Charts dealing with undesirable behaviours may simply say 'whenever the problem behaviour occurs' (followed by a precise description of the problem behaviour), or may relate frequency to certain levels of behaviour, e.g. 'whenever John is self-abusive'.

(7) Criterion for success

The purpose of this section is to define the level at which the new skill is taken as learned, or the problem behaviour is taken as permanently improved. Alternatively, this information can be included under the Teaching Objectives section. In the example Mary has to correctly complete five out of the six puzzles, and do this (or better) at every session for five consecutive days. The criterion for success might be higher (e.g. 100 per cent) for some programmes, or as low as 60 per cent for others. The deciding factor is each client's level of ability, concentration and motivation. It may be more important to encourage clients to participate than to insist on 100 per cent success, particularly in the early stages of a teaching programme.

In behavioural programmes the criterion for success may be expressed as a percentage reduction in the number of specified incidents, e.g. 'David will reduce the number of times he hits others by 25 per cent'. Usually this type of criterion only works with clients who have some degree of insight into their behaviour, and some motivation to change, e.g. tokens or payment. Criteria involving a reduction of behaviour can be expressed in one of two ways:

(a) Criterion = Previous level of behaviour minus 25 per cent.
(b) Criterion = Baseline behaviour minus 25 per cent.

However, although these two formulae appear to be similar, in practice they can produce quite different results. Starting with a problem behaviour that occurs 20 times per day, with option (a) the criterion for success for the initial programme would be 20 minus 25 per cent = 15; for the next programme the criterion would be 15 minus 25 per cent = 7.75, and so on. With option (b) the first programme would have the same criterion as option (a), but for the next programme the target would be lowered by 25 per cent of the baseline, i.e. another 5, giving a new target behaviour of 10. It does not matter in the least which option is chosen, as long as everyone involved understands what is going on!

(8) Reinforcement

Identifying the reinforcement and reinforcers used can be very helpful in confirming the type of approach that is to be used, and for showing how common composite teaching techniques are. In the example, Mary receives a direct reward for her achievement (positive reinforcement) and her reinforcer is a social one, verbal praise. This section can also remind staff to make sure that the appropriate reinforcers are available, particularly if primary reinforcers are being given.

(9) Equipment

This is a purely practical heading that reminds staff of the 'props' needed for the job.

(10) Procedure

This is the real heart of the programme, and should give the exact method of administration, presentation, correction and recording. It should also state in the first point whether or not teaching needs to take place in a particular room or area. Procedures should be written in numbered points, for ease of reference and administration, and each point should refer to a clearly defined part of the action. As far as is possible the procedure should be written as if verbal instructions were being given directly, in order to avoid the need to alter emphasis and tense when working with the client.

The procedure should include details about preparation and setting up, the ideal procedure to follow, what to do if problems occur, the order of work and how to record information. One of the commonest problems in writing charts is to omit seemingly obvious information (e.g. which hand the client is to use, assuming that everyone knows which is the client's dominant hand), only to find that a new member of staff needs that information to teach successfully. As a result, procedures can often appear to be over-involved and full of unnecessary detail, but this detail can be very important.

(11) Extra information

Staff carrying out training programmes may need more information or advice on what to do, so every chart should have details about where, and from whom, such information can be gained. The usual people to name are (a) to co-ordinator or key workers and (b) two or three other people who carry out the programme regularly. However, this section rapidly becomes unhelpful if names are not regularly updated!

(12) Recording chart

The recording chart is just as important as the teaching procedure, because it will hopefully reflect the changes that are envisaged. Recording charts are often the same as the baseline charts, and should always include a space for comments. The source of information entered should be identified by either initials or a name. Every recording chart should either be part of the teaching programme itself or be attached to it, and generally the simpler the chart, the more reliably it is filled in. Charts have to record either:

(a) simple success or failure at each task,
(b) every response to the procedure,
(c) the total number of successes during a session, or
(d) every correct response, where a number of correct responses are possible.

Charts can also be used as reinforcers in their own right with clients who respond well to visual feedback, by using stars on a bar chart, or by crossing out or highlighting areas of work that have been completed.

Figure 5.6: Example Activity Chart 2

NAME: Mary   TEAM AGREEMENT: 26.6.86
ADDRESS: DATE COMMENCED: 5.7.86
ACTIVITY: Reducing swearing
REASON FOR PROGRAMME: Mary swears to gain staff attention. She enjoys the reactions of the staff she has shouted abuse at, and this programme is designed to reduce the reinforcement that she receives for this behaviour (using extinction), while teaching her more appropriate ways of gaining the attention she wants.
WHEN TO USE THE PROGRAMME: Every time that Mary swears or is verbally abusive (see separate sheet for list of common phrases used by Mary).
WHAT TO DO:
1. Whenever Mary swears at you, or is verbally abusive to you, physically turn away from her and, if at all possible, find another client or member of staff in the immediate area to talk to. While you are doing this Mary should be 'invisible' to you, i.e. don't watch her, talk to her or react to what she is saying or doing.
2. Continue doing this until Mary's swearing and shouting stops. Mary's swearing and shouting may well get worse while you do this, but she won't harm herself.
3. When her swearing and shouting stops, go back to her and involve her in any positive activity that she likes, e.g. playing records, dancing or playing cards. Tell her how nice it is to be with her.
   N.B. As well as carrying out this programme, respond positively to Mary whenever she approaches you appropriately, or talks to you without swearing or shouting.
INFORMATION: For more information see Anne Potts, Swee, Chris or Niki.
RECORDING CHART:
Mark every time that you have to ignore Mary on the attached chart.

Date	Time	Approx Duration	Comments	Name

Figure 5.7: Example Activity Chart 3.

NAME: Jimmy
ACTIVITY: Toothbrushing
AIM: Jimmy is following a programme to increase his self-care skills. He
has some of the component skills required for toothbrushing, but needs
to link them with other parts of the task that he has not yet learned.
EQUIPMENT: Electric toothbrush with adapted handle, toothpaste, glass.
PROCEDURE:
1. Stand Jimmy in front of the washbasin.
2. Proceed through the stages in the chart below:

	Done by you	*Done together*	*Done by Jimmy*
a.			Pick up toothbrush
b.	Unscrew cap on toothpaste		
c.		Squeeze toothpaste onto brush	
d.	Screw cap on toothpaste		
e.	Switch on toothbrush		
f.			Lift toothbrush to mouth
g.		Brush teeth	
h.	Switch off toothbrush		
i.			Rinse toothbrush
j.			Put down toothbrush
k.		Rinse mouth	

NB. For more information see Cathy, Gill or Nick.

RECORDING CHART: Keep notes about progress in diary attached to this
programme.

SUMMARY

Most individual teaching requires a chart of some kind, and the more
detailed the chart, the more consistent the training is likely to be.
However, presenting information in a technical format, which
includes unfamiliar jargon, may be off-putting for people who have
no previous experience of working with such charts. If this is so, all
the benefits of a well-written programme will be lost if no one uses
it! The formal system of writing charts described earlier in this
chapter is useful for any programme writer to follow, but the type
of format adopted will depend on who is going to implement the
programme. The eventual style chosen will probably fall somewhere
between the very formal and the more informal example charts in
this chapter. In the final analysis, it is the success of the teaching that
is important, not the style of the written programme.

Further information

S. Bluma, J. Shearer, A. Frohman and J. Hilliard, *The Portage Project* (Co-operative Educational Service Agency, Wisconsin, 1976).

F.P. Connor *et al.*, *Program Guide for Infants and Toddlers with Neuro-Motor and Other Developmental Disabilities* (Teachers College Press, New York, 1978).

M. Bender *et al.*, *Teaching the Moderately and Severely Handicapped*, vol. 1, *Behaviours, Self Care and Motor Skills*; vol. 2, *Communication, Socialisation, Safety, Leisure-time and Functional Academics* (University Park Press, Baltimore, 1976).

L. Dunn *et al.*, *The Peabody Language Development Kits* (NFER-Nelson, Windsor, 1981).

H.D.B. Fredericks *et al.*, *The Teaching Research Curriculum for the Moderately and Severely Handicapped*, vol. 1, *Gross and Fine Motor Skills*; vol. 2, *Self Help and Cognitive Skills* (Charles C. Thomas, Springfield, Illinois, 1980).

M. Frostig *et al.*, *The Frostig Programme for Individualised Training and Remediation in Visual Perception* (Follet Publishing Co., Chicago, 1973).

S.H. Haskell and M.E. Paull, *Training in Basic Cognitive Skills: Training in Motor Skills* (Educational Supply Association, Essex, 1973).

D. Jeffree *et al.*, *Teaching the Handicapped Child* (Souvenir Press, London, 1977).

V. Johnson and R. Werner, *Step-by-Step Learning Guide for Retarded Infants and Children* (Constable, London, 1980).

V. Johnson and R. Werner, *Step-by-Step Learning Guide for Older Retarded Children* (Constable, London, 1980).

P. Saunders, *Micros for Handicapped Users* (Helena Press, Whitby, Yorkshire, 1984).

6

Developing Basic Living Skills

Basic living skills must be mastered before independence can be acquired.

All training aims to enable each person to live a life that is as independent and fulfilling as possible. The acquisition of independent living skills is a broad and complex training area, and if one area is emphasised more than another, imbalance in abilities occurs, so before planning and implementing a balanced and appropriate independent living skills training programme, it is essential to check whether or not the client has the skills necessary for participation. Kiernan[1] suggests that there are four factors which should be considered:

(1) *Rewards* — does the client have any likes which can be used as rewards in training or teaching sessions?
(2) *Educational blocks* — has the client a behaviour or disability which hinders learning? For those who are unable to move independently, a programme can be devised to enable the client to experience various positions, but in other cases, e.g. involving self-mutilation, the first priority must be to deal with the problem behaviour, so that programmes which assist general development can be successfully implemented.
(3) *Socialisation and communication* — does the client respond to others? Can the client communicate his needs to others? If a client is to develop new skills, he must be able to communicate in some way, and be able to interact and respond to others,

however briefly.

(4) *Reach and grasp* — does the client reach for and grasp things? Acquisition of new skills is much more difficult if this ability is not present.

Perkins *et al.*[2] add that any intensive training or teaching should focus on the following abilities:

(1) Can a client sit at a table without any fuss?
(2) Does the client look at a person calling his name?
(3) Does the client look at objects when working with them?
(4) Does the client co-operate, i.e. do what is expected?

Clients may need to overcome difficulties in these skills before beginning any specific training programme, or participating in a living skills training timetable. This may involve assisting clients to progress developmentally until they reach a stage where they have the necessary skills, or may require other solutions to permanent problems. Computers and other electronic learning aids can often enable a profoundly handicapped person to participate in training programmes, by using adapted input devices. Computers are also developing more and more applications for all individual teaching programmes, and may well be more reinforcing to a client than conventional teaching media. Irrespective of the means used, however, once the skills (or alternative methods of learning) have been mastered, independent living training can begin.

Independent living training needs to be made up of progressively more complex, but interrelated areas, and the process of acquiring independence can be divided into three broad training levels — basic, intermediate and advanced. Training may also need to include activities to maintain and/or consolidate existing skills.

Basic living skills are those which are necessary to use the body, to make needs known, and to learn — i.e. physical functioning and mobility, hand function, sensory understanding and communication. Skill in all these areas allows clients to participate in, and interact with, their environment and social group, and provides the basic building blocks for the development of personal care and self-help skills.

Intermediate living skills are those which apply basic control, function and communication skills to daily life. This means that intermediate training is made up of perceptual/conceptual understanding, play/recreation, and self-help skills (e.g. washing, dressing, feeding and toileting). Clients who have mastery of intermediate living skills will be able to independently care for themselves, apply their communication and interaction skills in a socially acceptable manner in order to have their needs met, and exchange information with others. However, intermediate clients still need high levels of support to maintain this degree of independence.

Advanced living skills are those which make it possible to live independently in the community, and to maintain a home (e.g. home-care, cooking meals, shopping, use of community facilities, travel and money management). This is one of the most complex of all training levels as every client has to develop not only a range of complex skills and behaviours, but also the ability to deal with unforeseen problems or emergencies. General principles can be given for this level of training, but ultimately each programme needs to be tailored to each client's needs and future living arrangements.

Maintenance activities are required for those who, temporarily or otherwise, are making little active progress but have skills that need to be maintained for as long as possible. Ability levels in this category may vary considerably, and a wide range of experiences and activities may need to be included.

To provide effective training, each level of living skill should have timetables of group work and individual work, related to the needs of the client group. In practice very few people fit precisely into only one level of training; more usually clients take training opportunities from two or even three training timetables, and so create their own individual training programme. This chapter, together with Chapters 7 and 8, looks more closely at the concepts of basic, intermediate and advanced living skills. However, each area cannot be fully dealt with within one chapter, and therefore additional information can be gained from the references at the end of each chapter.

BASIC LIVING SKILLS

People who need basic living skills training usually have both physical disabilities and learning difficulties, so in order to facilitate the skills which are usually acquired between birth and 5 years, staffing levels need to be high, and staff need to have a sound knowledge of normal child development. In normal development each child passes essential milestones (Figure 6.1), and these can be

Figure 6.1

Essential milestones

Birth	Prone — pelvis high, knees under abdomen.
	Ventral suspension — elbows flex, hips partly extended.
4–6 weeks	Smiles at mother. Vocalises 1–2 weeks later.
6 weeks	Prone — pelvis flat.
12–16 weeks	Turns head to sound. Holds object placed in hand.
12–20 weeks	Hand regard.
20 weeks	Goes for objects and gets them, without them being placed in the hand.
26 weeks	Transfers objects, one hand to the other.
	Chews.
	Sits, hands forward for support.
	Supine — lifts head up spontaneously.
	Feeds self with biscuit.
9–10 months	Index finger approach.
	Finger–thumb opposition.
	Creeps
	Pat-a-cake, bye-bye.
	Helps dress — holding out arms for coat, foot out for shoe, or transferring object from hand in order to insert hand in sleeve.
13 months	Casting (ceases by about 15 months).
	Walks, no help.
	Two or three single words.
15–18 months	Domestic mimicry.
15 months	Feeds self fully if given a chance, picking up a cup, drinking, putting it down without help.
	Casting stops. Mouthing stops.
18 months	Begins to tell mother about wetting.
21–24 months	Joins two or three words together spontaneously.
2 years	Mainly dry by day.
3 years	Mainly dry by night.
	Dresses self, except for buttons at back, if given a chance.
	Stands momentarily on one foot.

Source: R.S. Illingworth, *The Development of the Infant and Young Child* (Churchill Livingstone, Edinburgh and New York, 1985).

used as informal and approximate reference points when dealing with the problems that clients experience. In developmental terms, basic living skills training mirrors normal development between birth and 5 years.

The remainder of this chapter looks more closely at certain areas found within basic living skills, i.e. physical ability, hand function, sensory development and communication.

Many skills within these four functional areas can be helped by the provision of aids and/or specialised equipment, but the provision of any equipment needs specialist advice, as mistakes can be expensive and potentially make the client more dependent than is necessary. So, before giving anyone any aids/equipment, the following questions should be satisfactorily answered:

> Could the client be helped to achieve the same results without special equipment?
>
> If special assistance is required, could any existing aids or equipment the client has be adapted to provide the support needed?
>
> Is the assistance needed temporarily or permanently?
>
> Does the aid/equipment assist carers in the daily management of the client?
>
> Is the home environment suitable for the suggested aids/ equipment?
>
> Who will monitor its use, and make modifications when necessary?

There are a number of publications which deal with the use of aids and equipment, and the techniques for easier management of physical disability. This book does not include very much specific information about handling and lifting because (a) there are already books available that describe what to do, and (b) we feel that these practical techniques should be learned under the supervision of an experienced person. Equally, the suggestions made throughout this chapter (which apply to children, adolescents and adults) should be supplemented by further reading and by working alongside an experienced practitioner.

PHYSICAL ABILITY

Basic physical ability is made up of a range of abilities which can collectively be called the basic motor skills. These abilities are:

(1) head and trunk control
(2) symmetry
(3) rotation
(4) extension of the elbows
(5) balance
(6) flexion of the hips
(7) grasp and release.

Clients may well have disturbances in their muscle tone, e.g. spasticity, flaccidity, athetosis, or ataxia. Normal muscle tone describes the state of the body when tension is sufficiently high to withstand the pull of gravity (i.e. the body is kept upright), yet low enough not to interfere with intended movement. Spasticity is an undue resistance to changes of posture, or delayed adjustment of the muscles to postural change. Flaccidity is an undue lack of resistance, and hyperextension of joints during changing postural patterns. Athetosis and ataxia produce different movement patterns. Athetosis is characterised by continuous and uncontrolled movements, with intermittent undue resistance of the muscles to postural changes alternating with complete absence of resistance. Ataxia is characterised by movements that are jerky, poorly timed, poorly graded and poorly directed, with poor balance.

There are also postural reflexes, i.e. righting reactions and equilibrium reactions. Righting reactions are automatic, active responses which maintain the position of the head in space, and the alignment of the head to the neck and trunk, and the trunk to the limbs. Equilibrium reactions are also automatic responses, but they enable the body to maintain its balance throughout movement. By maturity these postural reflexes reach such a degree of refinement that it is possible to maintain body posture (balancing head, trunk, and lower limbs) while the hands and arms are engaged in skilled manipulative activities. This level of skill is, in normal development, achieved through a well-ordered sequence of events. From birth onwards, as the central nervous system matures, movement patterns gradually develop from the primitive reflex actions of the newly born infant, into the great variety and selectivity of the actions of a physically mature adult. However, mature movement patterns are achieved not only by the development of new skills, but also by the suppression of redundant reflexes, e.g. a young child who initially holds a building brick between its fingers and the palm of its hand (grasp reflex), has to learn to inhibit this response in order to be able to develop a tripod or pinch grip.

Clients who are developmentally delayed need a combination of the encouragement of appropriate skills with the discouragement of inappropriate reflex activity to enhance their physical development. Appropriate training activities can be planned in conjunction with various developmental primers (e.g. Sheridan[3]) but working on inappropriate reflex activity needs more specific knowledge.

Common reflex problems

All reflexes are designed to assist the newborn child to survive in what can be a hostile environment and, as stated above, functional problems can be caused by the continued presence of this reflex activity. Commonly seen reflexes are described below.

Asymmetrical tonic neck reflex (ATNR)

This reflex is elicited by rotating the neck. If the head is turned to the right, the right side limbs extend and the left side limbs flex slightly, with the arms being more affected than the legs. The position reverses if the head is turned to the left. This reflex is present in normal development until 4–5 months. If the reflex continues to be present after 4–5 months, clients are unable to:

(1) follow objects beyond the midline;
(2) roll over, pull themselves up to the sitting position, crawl, sit or stand;
(3) bring the hand to the mouth for feeding;
(4) reach or grasp and simultaneously look at an object.

In addition, clients tend to use only one hand, and repeated movement to one side of the body can lead to scoliosis, and the possible subluxation of the opposite hip.

Symmetrical tonic neck reflex (STNR)

This reflex is similar to ATNR, except that its effects are produced by extending or flexing the neck. Raising the head produces increased extensor tone in the arms and increased flexor tone in the legs; lowering the head produces the opposite effect. If this reflex continues, an affected client will be unable to:

(1) weight-bear simultaneously on the arms and legs — any attempt to crawl results in the client lying on his stomach with his legs extended;
(2) move the arms and legs reciprocally for crawling.

An individual may only be able to sit comfortably by kneeling with his bottom between his heels, and prolonged use of this position may lead to contractures.

Tonic labyrinthine reflex

This reflex is elicited by changes in the position of the head, and is common in the first few months of life, after which it comes under the conscious control of the client. Individuals affected by this reflex are unable to:

(1) (in the supine position) raise the head, play with the hands together, or roll into the prone position;
(2) (in the prone position) raise the head and turn to the side because the arms are caught beneath the body.

When supine, this reflex causes full extension, but when prone, extension is minimal and the client appears flexed.

Associated reactions

Associated reactions are probably the most important of all the abnormal tonic reflexes. The association causes tonic reflexes to spread from one limb to the rest of the affected part of the body; i.e. if a hemiplegic child squeezes a rubber ball with the sound hand, there will be an increase in the spasticity and accentuation of the hemiplegic pattern in the other hand. As physical stimulation or effort provokes the reaction, functional ability may be affected or restricted.

Positive supportive reactions

These are characterised by the simultaneous contraction of all the muscles in a limb, which makes that limb rigid and pillar-like. It can be provoked by tactile contact (e.g. by the touch of the ball of the foot on the ground) or by proprioceptive contact (e.g. by the pressure resulting from the stretching of the intrinsic muscles of the foot). Individuals affected by positive supporting reactions will:

(1) have a small weight-bearing base;
(2) find forward transference of weight difficult if the body is thrown backwards into extension;
(3) find heel–toe gait very difficult because of the restricted ankle movement;
(4) find graded weight-bearing difficult;
(5) have poor balance reactions.

Moro reflex

This is normal in children of up to 4 months. It can be elicited in the sitting position by flexing the head and then allowing it to fall

81

backwards; the client will initially extend and abduct the arms, and then return them to a flexed position. Affected clients will:

(1) have some interference in balance;
(2) have general performance affected through interference with hand function.

Grasp reflex

This is again normal in children of up to 4 months, and there are two stages to the reflex. Firstly, when the palm is stimulated by introducing a finger or object from the ulnar side, the fingers will flex and grasp whatever has been placed in the palm. The head is usually in mid-line, and the child finds it difficult to release whatever is held. Secondly, once the grasp reflex has been elicited and the grasped finger/object is drawn gently upwards, away from the child, a full-term baby will strengthen its grasp. There is progressive tensing of the muscles from the wrist to the shoulder, until the child momentarily hangs from the finger/object it has grasped. An affected client will:

(1) experience difficulty in grasping and releasing objects;
(2) have functional independence affected by the continuance of primitive grasp;
(3) have limited opportunities for perceptual and tactile exploration.

Sucking reflex

This is a reflex which can be automatically elicited by inserting a finger, nipple or feeding bottle teat into a baby's mouth. This is useful as long as clients are dependent on liquid food, but continuation of this reflex severely affects normal feeding. Inhibition of this reflex is needed to allow the use of the tongue to develop, and without this inhibition even spoon-feeding is difficult to achieve.

Rooting reflex

This is often called the seeking reflex, and helps a baby to find its mother's nipple, or a bottle teat. When the baby's cheek is touched it automatically turns its head towards the source of the contact. If this reflex activity continues, feeding and positioning for feeding can be affected.

Parachute reflexes

These reflexes appear between 6 and 9 months and persist through normal life. They are self-protection mechanisms, i.e. whenever the body falls forward, or is suddenly sent off-balance, the arms are extended in the direction of the fall, to prevent or minimise impact. The reflexes can be elicited by holding a child in the prone position, then suddenly lowering the child towards a table. Clients who fail to develop these reflexes are very vulnerable to accidents in daily life. Additionally, the absence of these reflexes may indicate an inability to weight-bear on the arms and hands, and may prevent clients from reaching out towards objects.

Landau reflex

This is similar to parachute reflexes both in form and effect, and is present in normal development after the age of 3 months. The reflex can be elicited by holding a child in the prone position and flexing its neck; the hips, knees and elbows flex when the head is flexed, protecting the front of the body. Failure to develop this reflex leaves clients unable to protect themselves, and if it prevents adequate extension of the neck, spine and hips, can prevent standing and walking.

Training suggestions

Any client who participates in a basic living skills training programme is likely to require special handling and positioning techniques in order to gain the maximum amount of benefit from their experiences. Correct management can enable clients to participate more fully in activities, and can prevent problems such as contractures from developing. Appropriate handling and positioning also helps to minimise the influence of abnormal reflexes and reactions. More specific management techniques, such as those outlined in the neurodevelopmental approach, can be used for specific clients, but the suggestions given below are principles for general use.

Supine

Lying supine is the most basic physical position, and is also the position of greatest helplessness, i.e. it is difficult to observe the environment, manipulate an object effectively in the mid-line position or to perceive and learn. Each client who is unable to move independently should experience a variety of different positions every day, and if left in the supine position for any length of time should be provided with visual stimulation, e.g. mobiles, ceiling pictures, or suspended objects. However, rather than leaving clients supine, use a back support or foam wedge (or anything that has a slight angle) to raise them into a position from which they can observe their surroundings. Positioning a client against a wedge overcomes the problem of hyperextension by flexing the hips, and positioning can be further improved by using a foot box. If the clients are positioned so that their feet are in contact with the foot box (with their ankles at an angle of 90 degrees), they are assuming a position similar to that used in standing, and preventing the shortening of the extensor tendons. (Foot boxes should be used whenever necessary.) In this position, knees can either be kept straight with gaiters, or flexed.

Prompt elbow extension in movements both towards and away from the mid-line, and encourage the client to maintain elbow extension from pronation to supination and vice-versa. Then encourage the client to use this skill, together with grasp and release, to assist in sitting up using a wooden stick. Being able to grasp the stick and maintain elbow extension, while being pulled to the sitting position, is an early stage in learning to move to the sitting position independently.

Keeping the client's knees flexed and his feet flat on the floor, encourage the client to raise the hips high enough above the floor to allow a small object to be passed underneath. The client may initially require support in raising his hips, but once learned this exercise is very useful in relation to (a) assisting in dressing/undressing procedures, and (b) learning to carry out parts of self-help procedures, e.g. removing lower limb clothing.

Early independent movement can be encouraged by teaching the client to throw one arm across the body, to provide enough momentum to assist in rolling.

Side-lying

Side-lying is a more useful position, combining a secure posture with the ability to participate and manipulate. (Side-lying boards can be used with those who are unable to stay in this position without support.) Individuals should be encouraged to move from supine to side-lying by flexing the right hip and knee (or vice-versa) and crossing the flexed leg over the body at the same time as throwing the right arm across the body. Individuals who can move from supine to side-lying in this way have achieved the first level of physical independence.

Prone

This position helps the client to develop head control, strengthens back muscles, stretches the hips and encourages weight-bearing, initially on the elbows, and ultimately on the whole arm. Place the client over a foam wedge or pillow, making sure that his arms are abducted from the body with the elbows at right angles if possible. The shoulders and arms should be externally rather than internally rotated, the head and trunk aligned, and the legs apart (internally rotated at the hips) with the knees straight. Introduce visual and auditory toys to encourage the client to raise his head, and to look at and follow the objects or sounds. As head and back control progresses, the client will be able to lift his head, raise his shoulders and chest, and rest his body weight on the forearms. Subsequently, weight can be taken through his hands and extended arms, and ultimately weight can be taken by either arm while the other reaches for and grasps objects. The activities carried out in the prone position, therefore, should always encourage upper limb weight-bearing.

Push the sole of each foot alternately and, keeping the leg externally rotated, slide the leg upwards flexing the knee and keeping the ankle at 90 degrees (i.e. similar to leg action in breast stroke swimming). Encouraging the client to do this prepares him for crawling. When ready to progress to crawling, prompt the client to weight-bear on extended arms, and then, while supporting the client, hold and gently pull his hips backwards. This will automatically flex the hips and knees into the crawling position.

Once the client can maintain the crawling position with help, gradually withdraw your support so that the client can progressively bear more and more of his body weight in a stable manner. When weight-bearing is stable in the crawling position, prompt and support the client to weight-bear on only one arm at a time. As before, support should be gradually faded out and the client encouraged to weight-bear on alternate arms, reaching out and grasping objects with his free arm.

Sitting

The ability to sit makes it possible to carry out a variety of activities. Most importantly, self-care activities need stability in the sitting position for success. Using the various seating and body support systems that are currently available — e.g. moulded seats, cushions and inserts — clients with no trunk control can sit. However, for real functional independence, head and trunk control needs to be developed.

Practise pulling the client to the sitting position using a stick or cut-off broom handle. The client should first be passively pulled to the sitting position while the shoulders are supported, then encouraged to grasp the stick and be pulled to the sitting position. The stick provides some measure of security while in the sitting position, but can also gently move the client from side to side to practise balance. While the client is sitting up and holding the stick, encourage him to shuffle forwards and backwards on the floor. As work with the stick progresses, encourage the client to reach progressively further for the stick, before rising to the sitting position.

At the same time encourage the client to work as much as possible in a chair. Initially side supports may be needed, but ultimately each client should aim to sit independently in a chair which gives minimum support. If clients are sitting incorrectly, they may be functionally restricted because of the pressure created by uneven weight distribution and the associated problems of maintaining the mid-line position of the back and head. The correct position to sit in is:

bottom well back in the chair,
weight equally distributed,
head and back held erect and in mid-line,
trunk leaning slightly forwards,
hips flexed,
knees and ankles flexed at 90 degrees,
both feet flat on the floor, or on a foot box.

Anyone who is physically unable to achieve the correct seating position may need corrective seating cushions. If cushions are being provided for uneven distribution of weight then they should be wedge-shaped, with the thickest part of the wedge under the weight-bearing side, rather than vice-versa; this corrects the original imbalance in weight distribution, whereas placing the thickest part of the wedge cushion under the non-weight-bearing side perpetuates the problem. Headrests should be avoided unless support is really needed. Consolidate the ability to sit in a stable position by putting the client in a variety of seats, e.g. different chairs, stools, rocking chairs. Also encourage the client to swivel around on chairs and stools.

Standing

The ability to stand is obviously an important prerequisite for walking, but it is also an important exercise for those people who will never be able to stand or walk independently. Standing contributes to the stability of the hip and knee joints, and provides a different range of visual, sensory and social experiences. Both standing frames and tilt tables can provide standing experience for more disabled clients, but for those with the potential to stand and walk independently, the following exercises may be useful.

From the crawling position, place the client's hands on a low stable chair. When the client can kneel in this way without support, concentrate on developing balance and compensation movements by moving the chair slightly. Finally, positioning the feet correctly, encourage the client to push himself up into a supported standing position.

Kneel down, sitting on your heels, and sit the client on your knee. Place your hands on his knees and as you rise to an upright kneeling position, press downwards on the knees to bring the client to a standing position (for children only).

Using wall bars (or a suitable chair) place the client's hands on a bar parallel to the height of his shoulders, while he is kneeling. Prompt clients to pull themselves up into the standing position by 'climbing' up the bars as they rise, keeping their arms level with the shoulder girdle at all times. When standing, make sure that the client's feet are flat on the floor and his weight is equally distributed. The legs should be slightly flexed at the hips and knees, a little apart and externally rotated, with the trunk upright. When the legs are fully weight-bearing, gradually reduce the amount of support needed, until the client can momentarily stand unsupported. Teach the client how to sit from the standing position by reversing the order of the actions necessary to move from sitting to standing, and also teach the client to reach, bend, grasp and pick up objects from a standing position.

Walking

Walking is a complex motor skill requiring co-ordination, balance, perceptual skill and spatial awareness, and cannot be learned before standing and balancing have been mastered. Walking requires previously learned skills to be applied to ever-changing conditions, and clients must learn to cope with (and compensate for) a variety of environments while maintaining locomotion. In walking, the heel of the foot must touch the ground first. The weight is then transferred, in a rolling motion, along the outside to the ball of the foot, as the heel is raised from the ground. Propulsion forward comes from downward pressure through the ball of the foot, while the weight of the body is simultaneously thrown slightly forward. Exercise must encourage and develop this pattern of movement.

Stand or kneel behind the client, who is standing, with your hands on the outside of his hips. Gently sway the client's body from side to side, so that the body weight is being transferred from one leg to the other. Also stand the client with one leg slightly in front of the other, and practise the same exercise, transferring weight forwards and backwards as the client sways. Finally, combine the two and prompt the client to move one leg forward as he sways, then to transfer the weight on to that leg.

Ask the client to hold on to a bar or chair, or frame, and to keep his arms fully extended. Standing behind the client, and holding his waist and hips, press downwards slightly. Ask someone to move the bar, chair, or frame a little forwards, and prompt the client to take a step towards it. Repeat as often as required. Stand the client against a wall or firm supporting surface, and stand one step away. Encourage him to take a step towards you, supporting him if necessary.

To teach stair-climbing, place the client's right hand on the banister or rail, and, standing to the client's left side, hold his left hand. Move the left hand forwards and upwards, and prompt the client to put the left foot on the next stair. Prompt and encourage the client to pull himself upwards using both hands, and then to straighten/transfer the weight of his left leg on the higher step, so that the other leg is automatically brought up to the same step. Follow this procedure for stairs where the banister is on the right-hand side; reverse the procedure when the banister is on the left-hand side. To teach a client to go down stairs, work backwards through this procedure.

HAND FUNCTION

Hand function depends not only on the motor control of the trunk, shoulder girdle, arms and hands, but also on visual, perceptual and cognitive development. Hand function is made up of reach, grasp and release, and competence in the use of the hand is needed for stabilisation (when supporting the body weight on extended arms), for moving into different positions, for grasping, manipulating, communicating and walking. The most common problems in hand function are:

(1) general developmental delay;
(2) abnormal hand grasp with wrist flexion or thumb adduction;
(3) abnormal release with wrist flexion, or with the thumb adducted, flexed and opposed across the palm, or with ulnar deviation;
(4) related problems from abnormal posture.

Effective hand function is refined over many years of development, but in relation to meeting training needs, several general points are clear. Firstly, clients must always be encouraged to look at their hands, and any toy or object they are reaching for. It may be necessary to teach observation, tracking and scanning skills either before or alongside the development of hand function. Reaching, grasp and release practice should also be included in all daily living and training activities.

Activities should involve the use of the hands in different ways, e.g. in unilateral and bilateral work. Bilateral work should include (a) using both hands simultaneously in the same way, e.g. clapping; (b) using both hands simultaneously in related but different ways, e.g. tearing paper; and (c) using both hands simultaneously but in opposition, e.g. one hand stabilising paper while the other hand draws.

Correction of abnormal posture enhances the function of the arms and hands: similarly, corrected arm function patterns provide a better learning posture. Movements away from the body, such as reaching out, pushing or playing when the arms are extended, should be encouraged as this enhances hand function, while movements which involve the adduction of the arms to the body should be discouraged, especially for those with spastic motor problems.

Exercises to develop hand function should also be linked to other training areas in order to extend each client's understanding of their environment. Individuals should be encouraged to take objects to the mouth to suck, bite or chew, or to the nose to smell, and be prompted to use the hands to feel shapes, textures and temperatures. In addition they should be taught to grasp/listen and grasp/look. Lastly, all hand function training should be structured to allow the client to work towards achieving personal independence in as many areas as possible.

Training suggestions

General training needs to facilitate the development of a wide range of hand function skills. Clients need to develop the use of the thumb and index finger through activities such as finger painting, or thumb printing and the use of toys and games that work through the pressing of a button, e.g. Jack-in-the-box, bells, or touch-screen computer games.

Training sessions also need to work on a variety of grasps, e.g. cylindrical grasp, tripod grasp or pincer grasp, and on the opposition of the thumb and fingers. Spreading and closing the fingers is another useful exercise. More specific problems, such as abnormal grasp and release, need to be dealt with more precisely.

(1) *For abnormal grasp with wrist flexion.* Place toys/objects at wrist level, and as the client tries to pick something up, press gently downwards on the back of his wrist. Sometimes a wrist extension splint may be necessary. Hammering (e.g. using a peg and hammer set) is an activity which helps to develop wrist extension.

(2) *For abnormal grasp with adducted thumb.* Hold the client's hand with your thumb between his thumb and index finger, and the rest of your hand grasping the ulnar side of his hand. As objects are grasped, gently press down on the ulnar side of the client's hand.

(3) *For abnormal release with wrist flexion.* Help the client to press the back of his wrist against a firm surface, in order to achieve the extension needed for release.

(4) *For abnormal release with thumb adducted and flexed across palm.* Teach the client to supinate the forearm, as this makes adduction of the thumb easier, and so promotes release. Thumb splints may also be useful.

SENSORY DEVELOPMENT

Sensory development is vital in order for clients to be able to discriminate valuable, important or meaningful information from the environment. Information gained in this way is interpreted on two distinct levels. Firstly, the senses (sight, hearing, taste, smell and touch), acting as channels through which this important information can pass, identifying individual stimuli. On a higher level, the brain then processes and reacts to *patterns* of stimuli, and allows each client to filter out important information from a mass of data. This higher level of function is known as perception, and training in perception forms part of intermediate living skills. In basic living skills, clients need to learn to interpret single stimuli.

Sight

Apart from functional skills such as tracking and scanning, clients need to be responsive to light levels, shapes, colour, etc. Training activities and experiences should take place in environments that are visually stimulating, and which change regularly. Visual stimulation should not be limited to certain parts of the environment — the whole living and working environment should stimulate all areas of sensory development.

There are many activities that can be involved in training sessions, e.g. using a torch and/or coloured lights for tracking and visual stimulation, using toys that move or produce some kind of action, stand-up picture books, puppets or ribbon sticks. At this stage of training it is advisable to use only real or three-dimensional objects for training sessions: the ability to perceive and interpret two-dimensional representations of real objects may not yet be present.

Hearing

Hearing results from the changes in atmospheric pressure which create sound waves. The sound waves are converted into electrical impulses through the mechanisms of the ear, and problems in either the reception or transmission of sound causes hearing problems. Individuals need to be able to discriminate between different qualities of sound, as well as to understand the meaning of various words and phrases.

Any aural training can make use of a variety of sound discrimination equipment, such as cassette tapes, that are commercially available. Additionally, training activities should always draw attention to the qualities of any relevant sound, e.g. 'listen to the water dripping from the tap', and use any available toys/equipment to reinforce sound discrimination. Finally, the use of the human voice as a teaching tool should not be forgotten — either as a basic sensory stimulus, or as a medium which can be copied, and responded to.

Smell

Smell is one of the most primitive and most important of the senses, yet it is probably the most overlooked sense as far as training programmes are concerned. Smell can be involved in virtually all activities. Obviously, media such as cooking and gardening spring to mind as activities rich in olfactory experiences, but aromatic substances can be concealed in boxes or pieces of equipment, to provide unexpected sensory input in other types of activities. Toys or pieces of equipment that are shaken or manipulated can have a few drops of essential oils or perfume touched onto them, so that as they are used, they give off different smells, and many household substances are perfumed and provide inexpensive smells. Essential oils, smelling of fruits, vegetables or flowers, can be more expensive and difficult to find, but have a stronger, more lingering smell. Some oils can be bought from chemists; others can be ordered through local or national associations for the blind.

Taste

Basic qualities of taste are sweet, sour, salt and bitter, and most tastes are made up of a combination of these four qualities. Information about taste is channelled through approximately 10,000 taste buds on the human adult tongue, but taste alone has limitations as a means of gathering information. Without smell and taste working together, the accuracy of taste identification diminishes. Teaching programmes therefore needs to combine, or work jointly on, taste and smell training.

In basic living skills training any tasting experience should be prefaced by the involvement of smell, and any work on smell should be followed (where relevant) by tasting. Where food preparation takes place away from the living environment, clients may need to be prompted to connect a smell with certain types of food. Smell, for example, can tell us when to avoid eating something, and when it is safe to taste, and clients need to be able to discriminate smells for their own protection.

Touch

Touch is not a single sensation, but has four basic components (touch, pain, warmth and cold) which are distributed in sensitive spots throughout the skin. These are not distributed evenly: pain spots are most frequent, followed by touch spots, cold spots and warm spots.

In everyday life any feeling is made up of a combination of the four sensations. Individuals need to be able to identify and discriminate each of these four sensations, and training activities should involve tactile exploration of the environment, tactile exploration of the body, comparing and contrasting different tactile experiences, and identification of objects through tactile clues only.

There is one remaining area that sensory development needs to include, and that is spatial awareness, or kinesthesia. As the body moves, sense organs in the ear (the semicircular canals and vestibular sacs) relate its current position in relation to gravity with the desired mid-line upright position. These organs identify the degree of disturbed equilibrium, or increased speed, that the body is experiencing, and if necessary allow the body to take corrective action. Experience at coping with changes in equilibrium comes through movement, and if clients are unable to move independently they may have limited experience of this, and consequently of spatial awareness. Training should therefore include opportunities for clients to experience changes in equilibrium and increase their spatial awareness skills.

Traditionally, this type of experience has been provided through playground equipment, swimming, and other outdoor activities, but new pieces of equipment such as inflatables to bounce (or be bounced) on, water mattresses, soft play equipment and ball pools provide a greater range of readily available experiences. Much of the experience gained on inflatables and in ball pools is caused by another person's actions, thereby adding a degree of unpredictability to these kinesthetic experiences.

COMMUNICATION

In normal development the drive to communicate is present from birth, and follows a fairly regular course. First vocalisations occur at about 6 months, and by about 4½ years most children have mastered the basic grammar and structure of mature speech. Competence in communication involves both learning and maturation, and is affected if learning difficulties or developmental delays (or both) are present.

Clients may have to cope with two levels of disability. Firstly, they may have communication difficulties because of learning or developmental problems, and secondly their access to, and interaction with, appropriate models of communication may be restricted. Despite these difficulties, however, the drive to communicate is still present, and no one should assume that communication is not important to a person who has difficulty in initiating interaction. A child learns to listen before learning to speak, and general therapeutic activities should therefore stimulate receptive understanding. This may involve descriptive conversation, action songs and rhymes, auditory games or auditory experimentation.

Any client with communication problems should have access to a speech therapist, and training programmes need to incorporate any remedial or teaching exercises that are recommended. In addition, signing systems may also need to be taught to non-verbal clients. Three well-known examples of communication systems are Bliss symbolics, Makaton, and the Paget-Gorman signing system.

Bliss symbolics

Blisss symbolics are standardised line drawings or representative pictures and concept devices which can be used singly or as composite signs. For example, a chair is represented by a side view of an upright chair, (showing two legs, a seat, and a chair-back), water is an undulating horizontal line, and a chair with water underneath it is a toilet! The symbols are drawn onto a squared chart (the number of squares/symbols depends on the ability of the client) which is kept near or in front of the client so that the symbols can be pointed at to initiate conversation or to answer questions. The word or concept represented by each symbol is written below it on the chart, so even those unfamiliar with the system can understand what the client is saying.

Makaton vocabulary

The Makaton vocabulary is a signing system which is, in essence, a simplified form of the British Sign Language for the Deaf (BSL). The vocabulary consists of 350 signs that are divided into nine teaching levels. Many of the signs make use of natural gestures which may already be understood, but the association between other signs and their meanings has to be taught. The vocabulary has to be used concurrently with speech/conversation because, with the limited number of signs in the vocabulary, only the key words are signed. For example, the sentence 'I'm going home for my dinner' is actually signed 'I go home my dinner'. The system is an additional communication method, not one which replaces normal speech.

Paget-Gorman signing system

This signing system was designed as a very comprehensive communication system for handicapped people. It contains approximately 3,000 signs and is a much more grammatically correct system, containing signs for the indefinite article and verb endings such as 'ing' and 'ed'. The signs are made by a series of hand and finger postures, and may rely on the composite use of two signs to form a new word, i.e. garage = building + vehicle.

Like the Makaton vocabulary, the Paget-Gorman system needs to be accompanied by normal speech, and its biggest advantage is that is readily teaches clients about the structure of spoken English. However, it does require higher conceptual abilities than other signing systems, and if clients are unlikely to become fluent in its use, then Makaton is a more realistic alternative. Because of this its use may be more limited: it is more commonly used by people following intermediate and even advanced training programmes.

Before starting to learn a signing system, clients must be able to copy actions and gestures. If they are unable to do this, then they should follow a pre-teaching imitation programme. The value of any signing system is dependent on the number of people who are proficient in its use. (Bliss symbolics are the exception, for the reasons given earlier.) A signing system is of little use to a client if only one or two others (either other clients or staff) are proficient in its use. This means that if signing systems are being taught to clients, staff must also be willing to learn, practice and regularly use the same system.

If clients have developed speech, no matter how limited this may be, training programmes need to provide opportunities for developing verbal communication patterns. Common problems at this stage may be poor articulation and expression, limited vocabulary and poor descriptive ability. Any activity can include descriptive and comparative vocabulary, e.g. 'the ball is round and bounces', or 'the black and white dog is bigger than the brown dog', but initial learning and teaching of these concept words is easiest through individual programmes.

SUMMARY

The teaching of basic living skills occupies a large proportion of the training time of any training programme. The ability to use and coordinate basic living skills takes time to develop, and intensive staff input to achieve. This need for comprehensive resources can seem difficult to justify for clients whose disabilities make it unlikely that they will ever achieve true independence, but basic living training provides the foundation skills that not only give each client the opportunity to try to become more independent, but also lead to a higher quality of life.

References

1. C. Kiernan, *Analysis of Programmes for Teaching* (Globe Education, Basingstoke, 1981).
2. E.A. Perkins *et al.*, *Helping the Retarded — a systematic behavioural approach* (British Institute of Mental Handicap, Kidderminster, 1983).
3. M. Sheridan, *From Birth to Five Years: children's developmental progress* (NFER-Nelson, Windsor, 1973).

Further information

Physical Function

K. Bobath, *A Neurophysiological Basis for the Treatment of Cerebral Palsy* (Spastics International Medical Publications/Heinemann, London, 1980).
J. Bryce, 'Facilitation of movement — the Bobath approach', *British Journal of Physiotherapy*, vol. 58 (1972), pp. 403–7.
J. Bryce, 'The Management of Spasticity in Children', *British Journal of Physiotherapy*, vol. 62 (1976), pp. 353–7.

Chartered Society of Physiotherapists, *Handling the Handicapped* (Woodhead Faulkner, Cambridge, 1980).

C. Cunningham and P. Sloper, *Helping Your Handicapped Baby* (Souvenir Press, London, 1978).

P.A. Downie and P. Kennedy, *Lifting, Handling and Helping Patients* (Faber and Faber, London, 1981).

N. Finnie, *Handling the Young Cerebral Palsied Child at Home* (Heinemann Medical, London, 1974).

M.R. Fiorentino, *A Basis for Sensorimotor Development: normal and abnormal* (Charles C. Thomas, Springfield, Illinois, 1981).

B.A. Fraser, *Gross Motor Management of Severely Multiply Impaired Students*, vol. 1, *Evaluation Guide*; vol. 2, *Management* (University Park Press, Baltimore, 1980).

H. Healy and S.B. Stainback, *The Severely Motor Impaired Student* (Charles C. Thomas, Springfield, Illinois, 1980).

B. Holle, *Motor Development in Children — normal and retarded* (Blackwell Scientific, Oxford, 1976).

J. Hogg and J. Sebba, *Profound Retardation and Multiple Impairment* (Croom Helm, London/Aspen Publishers, Rockville, Maryland, 1986).

S. Levitt, *Treatment of Cerebral Palsy and Motor Delay* (Blackwell Scientific, Oxford, 1977).

L. Routledge, *Only Childs Play* (Heinemann Medical, London, 1978).

G.B. Simon, *The Next Step on the Ladder — assessment and management of the multi-handicapped child* (British Institute of Mental Handicap, Kidderminster, 1981).

A. Wisbeach, *Positions for Play* (The Toy Libraries Association, 1982).

R. York-Moore and P. Stewart, *Management of the Physically Handicapped Child*, Series no. 1: *Guidelines to Handling*, and Series no. 2: *Guidelines to Lifting, Carrying and Seating* (British Institute of Mental Handicap, Kidderminster, 1984).

Hand function

E. Cotton, *The Hand as a Guide to Learning* (The Spastics Society, London, 1981).

R.P. Erhardt, *Developmental Hand Dysfunction: theory, assessment and treatment* (Ramsco, Laurel, Maryland, 1982).

A. Richardson and A. Wisbeach, *I Can Use My Hands* (The Toy Libraries Association, 1976).

Sensory development

A.J. Ayres, *Sensory Integration and the Handicapped Child* (Western Psychological Services, California, 1979).

B. Brereton and J. Sattler, *Cerebral Palsy: basic abilities* (The Spastic Centre of New South Wales, Australia, 1967).

D. Morrison *et al.*, *Sensory Motor Dysfunction and Therapy in Infancy and Childhood* (Charles C. Thomas, Springfield, Illinois, 1978).

Communication

J. Cooper, *Helping Language Development* (Edward Arnold, London and Baltimore, 1978).

P. Hastings and B. Hayes, *Encouraging Language Development* (Croom Helm, London, 1981).

D. Jeffree and R. McConkey, *Let Me Speak* (Souvenir Press, London, 1976).

P.R. Jones and A. Cregan, *Sign and Symbol Communication for Mentally Handicapped People* (Croom Helm, London, 1986).

K. Leeming *et al.*, *Teaching Language Communication to the Mentally Handicapped* (Methuen, London and New York, 1980).

G.F. MacKay and W.R. Dunn, *Early Communication Skills* (University of Glasgow, 1981).

7

Developing Intermediate Living Skills

Intermediate living skills help clients to care for themselves with some
support

As clients progress and gain more functional control of their body,
intermediate training can begin. Intermediate living skills are those
which enable clients to care for themselves in a supportive environment, and are therefore largely concerned with independence in self-
care, understanding of the environment and living with others.
Clients for whom intermediate level skills will be their highest level
of achievement can live fairly independently in small residential
settings such as group homes, as long as the right level of support
is provided. When support is provided, it should encourage and help
whenever necessary, but should not take over responsibility for
decision-making and daily routines.

While intermediate living skills certainly enhance and extend
independence they do not, on their own, enable a client to live
outside a supportive residential unit. Intermediate skills are,
therefore, the means through which clients can achieve sufficient
independence to live with dignity in a sheltered environment, and the
foundation skills that more able clients need to progress further. The
areas covered by this chapter are:

(1) Perceptual and conceptual learning,
(2) Play and interaction,
(3) Self-care.

PERCEPTUAL AND CONCEPTUAL LEARNING

A client learns about the world through sensory experience, and the process of extracting information from sensory input is called perception. Perception, however, also makes use of past experience and present needs, and enables the client to form concepts. Perceptual skill is the process of interpreting the patterns of sensory stimuli that each client receives. Traditionally, perceptual ability is related to the five senses i.e.:

> sight, and visual perception;
> hearing, and aural perception;
> touch, and tactile perception;
> taste, and gustatory perception;
> smell, and olfactory perception.

The most commonly used areas of perception are sight and hearing, but very often perception involves a composite use of two or more senses working together. Perception also involves understanding the constancy of things that are perceived, i.e. object constancy, brightness and colour constancy, shape and size constancy or position constancy, and requires the client to analyse and give meaning to information that is apparently meaningless, e.g. figure/ground discrimination, visual illusions, apparent and real motion and depth perception.

A concept is an idea, symbol or stimulus that stands for objects or things. For example lady, drink, fruit, plant and red are all concepts that unite different people or objects within the same class. Concepts can equally apply to objects that are related in some way, e.g. longer, wider, bigger and stronger, or to abstract ideas such as honesty, time, fairness and God. Initially, concepts that are obviously demonstrable or concrete (e.g. boy) are easier to acquire, and in normal development children rapidly incorporate this sort of conceptual language into their speech. Concepts concerned with relationships and abstract ideas, e.g. good boy/bad boy, take longer to acquire, but any form of conceptualisation requires the client to generalise and discriminate.

TRAINING SUGGESTIONS

Many perceptual problems can be improved simply by facilitating appropriate experiences; a lot of perceptual learning is a result of exploration of the environment and interaction with a family group. Many clients are restricted by their disabilities from perceptual 'discoveries'; multiply handicapped clients may have to be actively prompted or given access to sensory experiences, while more able clients may need to be encouraged to develop through specific exercises and play activities.

In general, any textbook that explains the normal sequences of perceptual development can provide a structure or framework for planning perceptual training. More specific problems may be highlighted by assessments (e.g. Frostig[1]) and need particular action. For example, problems in the development of Gestalt may be highlighted by the Frostig assessment, and rectified by following the recommended remedial exercises. ('Gestalt' means pattern or configuration, and Gestalt psychology emphasises the importance of being able to perceive the whole as well as the individual parts of an object.) Other assessments also recommend remedial activities for areas of need, and the following ideas may also be useful.

Visual memory

It is easier for a client to retain and recall visual details if classification and discrimination have already been learned. Recall is also helped if the client is able to attach a verbal label to the various component parts of a learning process. An associated ability is closure, i.e. the ability to perceive and imagine missing parts.

Encourage clients to practise drawing shapes or figures from other drawings or pictures. Then show pairs of pictures to the client (some pairs of identical pictures mixed with pairs of non-identical pictures). After looking at the pictures, ask the client to say whether each pair is identical and if not, to identify the differences.

Using a series of pictures, each of which has hidden objects, ask the client to find and identify the items hidden in each picture.

Sequencing and scanning

In order to assimilate visual information the client has to learn to make logical sequences in a task, and to co-ordinate a series of discrete fixations into a useful skill, e.g. learning left–right tracking before reading. Try to establish either left or right dominance, and overall awareness of left and right.

Using a pegboard, prompt the client to complete a sequence of different colours (e.g. one green, one red, one green) horizontally and then vertically.

Prompt the client to carry on a sequence of dots from left to right, e.g.:

. .   . . or . . . .

Show a series of picture cards in a set order, e.g. a car, a house, and a cat, and then ask the client to arrange them in a correct order on the table working from left to right.

Clap a rhythmic sequence with your hands, or using a drum/tambourine. Ask the client to reproduce the sequence as accurately as he/she can.

Visual discrimination

Clients have to learn to make visual judgements about objects, e.g. similarities and differences. These visual judgements are used in a generalised manner to make decisions and choices in everyday life.

Ask the client to sort out objects or shapes by colour, type and shape. Then prompt the client to match three separate shapes with the same shapes represented on a piece of card.

Encourage the client to copy line patterns on a dot grid, progressing from simple shapes to complex patterns, e.g.:

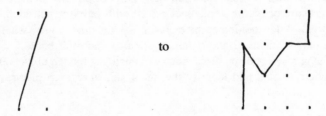

Draw a series of straight lines (matchstick length) and ask the client to copy each shape using matchsticks, e.g.:

Using cards in sets of three, ask the client to identify which of the three cards differs from the others in some way, e.g.:

Hand–eye co-ordination

This is the ability to look at an object and at the same time grasp the object and use it to perform a given task. Draw parallel lines of varying widths on a piece of paper and ask the individual to draw a line from left to right between the parallel lines, without touching them, e.g.:

or

Present a simple dot pattern to the individual and ask him to join the dots together into a given design, e.g.:

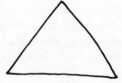

103

Take this a step further by using a pegboard to create patterns which the client then has to copy.

Draw various shapes on paper and ask the client to cut closely around each shape, cutting parallel to the lines drawn.

Concept acquisition can also follow normal development and teaching procedures, but each concept needs to be broken down into appropriately sized learning objectives, and learning must take place within an environment where there is:

(1) adequate freedom to explore and experiment,
(2) sufficient time to use and apply newly learned skills,
(3) reinforcement from good role models.

Conceptual learning is also consolidated in everyday interaction, daily routines and creative activities. This is advantageous as long as the same conceptual ideas are being reinforced by everyone concerned! For example, there is little point in one member of staff concentrating on discrimination between red and blue, while another member of staff is concentrating on discrimination between green and white, if all this does is confuse the client.

PLAY AND INTERACTION

Play and interaction skills (related to participation in activities) form the basis of a client's ability to learn relevant skills, and lay the foundations for the development of appropriate social and recreational competence.

Play is vital to people's development, helping them to master basic skills, expression, communication and spatial awareness. Young babies spend hours playing (kicking their legs, opening and closing their hands and feet, feeling their face with their hands) and gradually becoming more aware of the world by watching their mother, listening to her voice, smelling and tasting new food and feeling a variety of textures. When they begin to handle objects they learn more about size, shape, weight and texture.

As children become mobile they learn more about relative size, distance and spatial relationships, and take notice of the actions and speech of others. When play reaches an imaginative stage, language and role experimentation develop concurrently. Objects are not only interesting for their own sake, but can also take on imaginary shapes, roles and functions; dolls become real people, sand and water becomes food and drink, or chairs become trains. During imaginative play, children begin to learn to cope with emotion, to live and co-operate with others, and to refine functional skills that are likely to be mirrored in daily life.

Most children progress naturally through these stages, but handicapped clients may not be able to progress spontaneously from one level of development to the next. Conversely, clients may have the physical skills needed to participate in play activities, but need to be prompted to join in. Play in both instances should aim to stimulate and involve each client to the fullest extent.

Play opportunities also need to be extended to handicapped adults, if developmentally appropriate. Adults have the same needs as children, so they too should have access to play sessions and recreational activities. The only differences that may need to be considered are the age-appropriateness of resources used, and the adult size of equipment/facilities. However, although adult play should include child-like developmental work, the activities used should not be childish.

More sophisticated forms of play are called recreation, or leisure pursuits, and no clients should be prevented from participating in any activity that they find interesting and stimulating. By and large, clients who can actively pursue a hobby or leisure time interest are likely to be following an intermediate/advanced training programme. Intermediate clients are likely to need help in pursuing their interests, whereas advanced clients are likely to be independent.

TRAINING SUGGESTIONS

Firstly, select appropriate assessments to show each client's level of play skill development. Provide a wide variety of assessment situations and activities so that information gained is as comprehensive as possible. Then select activities that are both suitable for the client's current developmental level, and a little beyond it, covering all areas of function and ability.

Involve a variety of toys and interesting objects, and look at ways of using one object to develop different skills, e.g. nesting cups can be used for grasping, banging, building, colour recognition, and colour matching. However, unless a balance between familiarity and over-stimulation is achieved, the client will become bored, and play (above all) should be fun.

The next few pages (see Table 7.1) reproduce charts from the *Good Toy Guide*,[2] which gives various ideas for stimulating and developing play. The age levels at the top of each section are only intended to be an approximate guide to normal development. Obviously this chart was written specifically for use with children, but the play ideas can be adapted for use with clients of all ages.

Table 7.1:

When a child can:	Provide	To encourage
0–6 months		
Follows objects with eyes. Attention caught by sounds.	Mobiles to fix on cot — musical or silent. Baby mirror on side of cot.	Listening, eye movements and following. Attention to movement.
Kick legs.	Soft balls and foam bricks. Rattles with varying sounds.	Awareness of bodily movements.
Begin to reach and grasp (but cannot yet sit without support).	Toys to string on cot and pram. Small light rattles easily grasped by baby.	Aiming and grasping (baby associates movement made with the sound).
6–12 months		
Begin to put hands to mouth.	Toys that are light, safe, suitable for mouthing, e.g. teethers.	Discovery of mouth.
Sit supported at first and visually alert.	Toys with suction base that can be fixed on to play tray. Toys that can be hung where baby can reach and grasp. Toys that move easily when touched.	Hand–eye co-ordination. Child's activity produces a result.
Lie on tummy.	Toys that move when touched.	Movement in lying position, e.g. rolling over.
Sit with support.	Activity centres. Textured balls.	Exploration of a range of effects caused by hand movement. Exploration of textures using two hands.
Manipulate with fingers and use two hands together.	Objects that can be explored with fingers.	Co-ordination and two-handed play and five-finger movements.
Give and take objects.	Graspable objects that can be transferred from one hand to another, e.g. rattles, plastic cotton reels.	Practice in grasping and releasing. Bringing hands together in the middle. Giving and taking objects with adults.
12–18 months		
Spontaneously bang on the table.	Drum, xylophone, hammer toys.	More precise hand–eye co-ordination.
Crawl and push objects along.	Balls of various sizes. Various push-along toys, especially those on short rigid handles.	Increase in range of mobility and hence exploration.
Walk with support.	Baby walkers and other push toys on wheels.	Confidence and independence.
Walk without support.	Pull-along toys.	Co-ordination of body movements. Refinement of balance and walking skill.

Table 7.1: contd

When a child can:	Provide	To encourage
Imitate sounds. Understand simple phrases and words. Co-ordinate objects. (Relate objects to a container.)	Rag books and catalogues. Telephone. Baby mirrors. Plastic pots and pans. Simple posting boxes (i.e. with round and square shapes). Bricks and coloured cotton reels to put in and tip out. Large cardboard boxes and laundry baskets.	Simple imitation in a social context. Understanding of first picture symbols. Hand–eye co-ordination. Shape discrimination and putting into containers.
Begin to imitate parents' domestic duties.	Simple domestic items, broom, duster, plastic cup and spoon, hairbrush, flannel.	Simple representational play.

19 months–2 years

When a child can:	Provide	To encourage
Drum with two sticks.	Drums, xylophone and other 'banging' toys such as hammer pegs.	Hand–eye co-ordination and channel 'banging' into constructive activity.
Hold pencil.	Paper and jumbo pencil and crayon.	Improve hand–eye co-ordination. Scribbling and later copying.
Build several bricks into a tower. Use pincer grasp (and still preoccupied with container play).	Building beakers and other stacking toys. All toys using peg men.	Simple constructional activity. Refinement hand–eye co-ordination. Early representational play.
Enjoy simple picture books and other simple pictures.	Ladybird first books. Lift-out puzzles with pictures underneath. Inset puzzles.	Language development, and conversation.
Recreate domestic situation.	Simple domestic play, e.g. cookers and pans, doll's tea set. Cleaning sets. Little doll's pram or pushchair.	Early 'pretend' activities. Relating several 'pretend' items together.

2–3 years

When a child can:	Provide	To encourage
Push and pull large items. Climb steps with some agility.	Large push-along vehicles, trundle toys.	Climbing on and off. Over-coming problems of balance and steering.
Throw or kick a ball.	Large plastic skittles and ball. Football.	To help develop aim and possible turn-taking in games.
Begin to push and pull large toys skilfully and negotiate objects.	Wheelbarrow. Little doll's pram. Large lorries.	Development of skill in steering and symbolic play.

(By 3 years)

When a child can:	Provide	To encourage
Begin to pedal.	Tricycle.	Balance and good co-ordination.
Begin to master dressing skills.	Simple dressing-up items, cloaks, hats, accessories (without buttons).	Role play.
Assemble a screw toy.	Toys with screwing action.	Practice in this skill so that more advanced construction toys are possible.
Begin to copy simple figures and draw.	Chubby crayons and thick pencils.	Interest in drawing. Can then introduce templates and other tracing activities.

Table 7.1: contd

When a child can:	Provide	To encourage
Begin to match two or three primary colours and name them. Enjoy picture book, recognising fine details. Match four pictures.	Matching games using colour. Colour snap, colour matching dominoes. Simple picture lotto.	To learn concept of 'same' and 'different' and simple activities.
Can pour water from one cup into another.	Various containers for water play. Try funnel. Also water/bath toys.	Hand–eye co-ordination (especially two hands).

3–4 years

Push and pull large toys, while walking and running. Ride tricycles. Throw, catch and kick ball. Show agility in climbing.	Scooters and barrows. Tricycle and pedal cars. Football, games involving bat and ball. Access to climbing frame, ropes, etc.	Agility and balance. Confidence in agility. Muscular strength.
Cut with scissors.	Materials for cutting, sticking, collage.	Fine hand skills. Creative play.
Copy and trace shapes.	Wooden templates. Tracing activities.	Refinement in use of pencil and crayon.
Sort and compare materials. String beads. Complete more complex jigsaws.	Threading beads and sorting materials. Increasingly difficult puzzles.	Fine hand–eye skills. Fine discrimination. Simple shape and colour discrimination. Problem-solving and language development.
Show awareness of numbers.	Number dominoes and simple games involving dice.	Recognition of quantity. Simple games with rules.
Draw a simple person.	Paints, paper, brushes.	Creative and symbolic representation.
Make believe and show imaginative play, especially in social context.	Playgroup or other group experiences. More varied 'dressing-up'. Small representational objects — small dolls, people. Larger props for group domestic play. Shops.	Language development and social skills. Symbolic activity, planning more elaborate games.

4–5 years

Skip, hop.	Skipping rope and hopscotch mat.	Better co-ordination. Singing games, balance.
Copy shapes and letters.	Magnetic letters. Letter shapes. Chalk blackboard. Maze tracing.	Simple spelling and letter recognition. Precise control in 'writing'.
Plan and build constructively.	Layout and creative kits. Farm, zoo animals, Noah's ark. Playmats, garages, train layouts.	Practice in planning construction. Use of verbal skills to plan and explain actions to self and others.
Understand the rules of games — become competitive.	Simple competitive games — snakes and ladders, draughts, noughts and crosses, racing games, hide and seek.	Practice in 'winning and losing'. Strategy — taking the position of the other person.

For sports and recreational activities, high standards need to be set, and the correct equipment used. Non-sporting activities should also be offered as alternative interests; not everyone likes to pursue active hobbies/interests, and clients should therefore be encouraged to try a wide range of activities from traditional crafts to wine making, photography, country dancing and music making.

SELF-CARE

The terms 'self-care' and 'activities of daily living' (ADL) describe everything from the most basic to the most complex aspects of daily life. These activities need to build on perceptual/conceptual and play skills, and also require competence in the basic motor skills before real independence can be achieved. When teaching self-help skills the same basic principles apply to all areas of function, but the manner of implementation may differ. Most self-help skills are complex, composite actions, and they therefore need to be taught in a clear well-structured manner, i.e. following the teaching principles found in Chapters 3 and 5. The areas of self-care considered in this chapter are:

(1) dressing/undressing and clothes selection,
(2) toileting,
(3) management of menstruation,
(4) washing,
(5) hairwashing and styling,
(6) toothbrushing and denture care,
(7) shaving,
(8) appearance and grooming,
(9) eating and drinking.

Problems in self-care can only be solved within the confines of any physical disability. The provision of aids and pieces of equipment may increase the level of ability, but will not completely solve problems. Teaching should, ideally, be the result of careful assessment and planning, and related to known developmental performance in other functional areas.

1. DRESSING/UNDRESSING AND CLOTHES SELECTION

Both dressing and undressing should be taught in small steps. Undressing is easier to learn than dressing, so it is often the first skill taught. The most effective teaching technique to use is backward chaining, because it always repeats and reinforces the previously learned step(s). For example, in teaching a client to take off his socks, the first step to be taught is pulling the socks off the tips of the toes; clients then gradually work through to the last step of the programme which is taking the sock over the ankle, along the foot and off over the toes. After the first step has been learned, clients only have to work to the end of the newly taught step before revising a previously learned skill. Backward chaining works well with all dressing procedures.

In the early stages of teaching, encourage success by:

(a) Always describing exactly what is being done, even if the client has been successful, e.g. 'Well done . . . you've put the left shoe onto your left foot and the right shoe onto your right foot'. This reinforces correct identification and descriptive vocabulary.
(b) Use loosely fitting clothes that can easily be put on without help. Gradually introduce more and more fitted items of clothing.
(c) Choose clothes made from natural fibres to reduce the amount of static in clothing. (Static in clothes can make it difficult for a client to put on clothes correctly.)
(d) Use substitute fastenings if it makes learning easier, but then try to phase out their use in favour of more traditional fastenings.

Dressing, undressing and clothes selection consist of a series of linked sequences, which have to be learned individually before being combined together into independent functioning. These sequences are:

Functional sequencing: the patterns of movement required to put on and fasten (or undo and remove) individual items of clothing.

Serial order sequencing: the ability to identify garments and put them on in a logical and ordered sequence.

Co-ordination sequencing: the ability to choose matching and co-ordinating clothing to wear, and to know how to wear clothes to best advantage.

Appropriateness sequencing: the ability to choose appropriate clothing for age, activity or weather conditions, and to be aware when clothing should not be worn, e.g. when it is dirty.

Functional sequencing

Teaching the actual mechanics of dressing and undressing is always a slow progress, and is most efficiently managed using chaining, with shaping and prompting involved as necessary. Each dressing task must be broken down into its component parts, so that it can be taught by presenting one small part at a time. It is also important to remember that, when using chaining as a teaching technique, the chaining process should be applied to the whole dressing procedure and not repeated for every garment in turn. This might lengthen the time before achievement is seen, but the quality of learning is likely to be higher and the client likely to be less confused.

For upper limb garments

Always allow the client to sit near a table, or have a chair available, or put him into a side-lying position if their balance is poor but hip mobility good. For dressing, always try to minimise the number of different actions that have to take place at once; the greater the number of actions that have to be performed concurrently, the more concentration and co-ordination is required. Undressing is usually a simple reversal of the dressing procedures, and although it is obviously easier to pull an item off than to take it off correctly, clients should still be encouraged to undo fastenings wherever possible. Obviously, much of the dressing programme can be made easier if clothes are front-fastening, or open completely, but this is not always possible. For example, putting on a back-fastening bra can be difficult, and a simpler solution may be to buy front-fastening bras. Alternatively clients can be taught to do the bra up around their waist, and then pull it into position. Clothing might need to be adapted for specific physical problems, but generally alterations should be avoided as far as possible.

For lower limb garments

The client should be positioned as for upper limb garments, or should kneel or sit on the floor or bed. Clothing should be pulled over the feet and up to the knees before the client either stands or arches their back to enable clothing to be pulled up over the hips.

111

Again, clothing might need to be adapted for specific physical problems, but alterations should be avoided as far as possible. Managing fastenings such as laces, buckles, or buttons, should always be taught 'in situ' rather than on lacing or buttoning boards, in order to prevent the client from having to alter the plane in which the activity is carried out. Coloured insoles or clearly marked symbols can help clients to discriminate left and right when putting on shoes.

Serial order sequencing

This type of sequencing requires the client to be skilled in the identification of individual items of clothing, and in understanding the correct order in which to dress. Once the names of individual garments have been learned, they should be consolidated as often as is appropriate in the actual dressing task. Teaching dressing order requires some conception of the differences between underclothes and outer garments, and this can be achieved either through size or colour discrimination.

Sequencing by size can be successful if (a) visual perception is good and (b) standard clothing is worn. In the majority of instances the smallest items of clothing are put on first, and the largest last, and it is therefore not necessary for the client to be able to name each garment.

Sequencing by colour is an alternative that needs careful organisation, but if colour recognition is good it can be successful. This approach requires that all underclothes are white, while other clothes are coloured; the client starts dressing with white garments and progresses to coloured ones. In both suggested sequencing methods the client needs to lay out the selecting clothing so that correct choices can be made.

Co-ordination sequencing

Teaching clients to co-ordinate clothing is difficult, because inevitably the matter of personal taste impinges on teaching. Visual perception and recognition of colour and pattern are obviously important, and should be taught before any co-ordination sequencing programme is started. It is easier to start co-ordination sequencing by encouraging clients to keep to one colour when dressing, and to then progress on to co-ordinating different colours.

This area requires more verbal praise and feedback than others to overcome the inherent problems of there being no 'right' or 'wrong'. However, once someone has shown himself able to co-ordinate and colour match, then any subsequent co-ordination of clothes is more likely to be due to personal taste rather than lack of ability. Any co-ordination training should take place before dressing begins, and include the use of a full-length mirror.

Appropriateness sequencing

One of the last procedures in independent dressing training is to learn to choose clothing which is appropriate to age, activity and weather. Individuals may achieve independence in the mechanical aspects of functional, serial and co-ordination sequencing relatively easily, but still be unable to select clothes which are clean, suitable for the occasion, and practical for their lifestyle needs.

Choosing or identifying clean clothing, irrespective of colour and appropriateness, is often not so difficult to achieve as the others, because competence can be gained through following 'rules'. There are three levels to the recognition of dirtiness:

(a) recognition of sudden dirtiness, e.g. spilt food, paint, urine;
(b) recognition of cumulative dirtiness, e.g. dirt around collars and cuffs;
(c) recognition of unseen dirtiness, e.g. sweat.

Discrimination of the first two is relatively easily taught, and clients should learn to change their clothes whenever they recognise obvious dirt. Recognition of unseen dirt can be more difficult to teach, but can be solved by applying 'rules' for changing clothes regularly, e.g. after strenuous exercise.

Clothing which is not age-appropriate can rapidly single out a client as different, and clients therefore need to learn to choose and wear clothing that is appropriate to their age, and physical appearance. This needs to be handled sensitively, preserving clients' rights to make their own choices whilst helping them to assess suitable styles and clothing.

Other areas of appropriateness (weather and activity) are both complex skills because they require the client to make decisions based on unforeseen or future circumstances. Weather appropriateness

113

requires each client to recognise the current or future weather conditions and dress appropriately (or take appropriate items such as a jacket or umbrella). Clients may need to learn to use weather forecasts to help them make their decisions, but activity appropriateness requires clients to think ahead to decide what type of clothing they need to wear to meet the day's events. This may include taking sports clothing for an exercise session, or a change of clothing for social events after work. Some clients may find it helpful to have rough guidelines drawn up, e.g.:

    rainy weather = coat, boots, umbrella
    sunny weather = no coat, thin clothes, sunglasses
    cold weather   = jumpers, coats, hats, gloves, scarves
    gardening   = old clothes, wellingtons
    parties   = best clothes, jewellery
    shopping   = comfortable shoes, bags
    sport   = track suit, plimsolls, equipment, holdall

These informal guidelines not only help clients to make decisions about their clothing, but also make staff more consistent in the advice they give.

2. TOILETING

The bladder of a newborn baby is easily stimulated and its use is not under conscious control, but by approximately 1 year some association of ideas between urination/defaecation and the use of a potty has developed, and the child starts to indicate toileting needs by gesture. Not until the child is approximately 4 years old is toileting independence achieved. This gradual acquisition of independence can easily be upset by emotional stress, excitement, new surroundings and new experiences — e.g. attending school for the first time.

Toileting independence for clients may be considerably delayed because of general developmental delays, neurological problems or prolonged dependence on others. The best time to begin toilet training is obviously as near to the normal developmental time as possible, or when the client has achieved relevant developmental milestones. The easiest person to toilet-train is someone with regular toilet habits. Toilet training relies on the regular association of certain behaviours with urination and defaecation facilitating permanent changes in performance. In order to achieve this regular association, staff need to be able to predict with some certainty when a client needs toileting so that training can occur *before* the client urinates or defaecates. Training a client with irregular toilet habits is much harder because of the unpredictability about when toilet training will need to be implemented. In extreme cases toilet training may need to be carried out very frequently (e.g. every ½ hour) irrespective of whether or not the client actually urinates or defaecates.

The first essential in toilet training is to work from concrete data about the frequency of incontinent episodes, and this requires staff to collect baseline information for several weeks before implementing any sort of programme. Baseline information establishes whether incontinence occurs at particular times of the day or night (e.g. 1 hour after meals), how frequently clients visit the toilet, how frequently clients actually need to use the toilet, and how dependent on others they are. Record forms should be designed to obtain all this information quickly and easily, and to indicate priority areas for training. True independence requires each client to (a) recognise the need for toileting, (b) act upon this information in sufficient time to avoid accidental urination or defaecation, (c) use the toilet correctly, and (d) carry out personal hygiene procedures.

Clients who have continence problems are usually toileted regularly, so the first stage in training is often to encourage the client to take some responsibility for deciding when he needs to use a toilet. This could involve teaching 'toilet' signs to clients who are unable to communicate verbally, and teaching clients to recognise physiological signs. Enuresis alarms may be helpful at this stage in alerting clients either to ask for assistance or to attend to their needs themselves. Clients who fail to allow sufficient time to reach the toilet, yet can recognise appropriate physiological signs, may need to follow a behavioural programme that links rewards/privileges to high standards of continence. Token schemes can be effective in situations such as these, when clients receive praise and tokens for continence, and a neutral response (or even loss of tokens) for incontinence.

In addition to actually using the toilet appropriately, clients may also need to be taught how to transfer on and off the toilet, how to use toilet paper, and how to flush the toilet. Children may have trouble adapting to toilets (child or adult size) because of the difference in appearance and height, and in some cases refuse to use a toilet. Reassurance and physical support may help, but in persistent problems, shaping may offer the best solution. For example, by gradually changing the appearance and height of a potty, making it more and more like a toilet, much of a client's anxiety may be diffused. Similarly, shaping can be used to get clients used to using a potty in the bathroom, as a precursor to starting to use a toilet.

Personal hygiene procedures should be taught throughout toilet training programmes, even when clients are dependent on others. Hand washing is an obvious example; everyone should wash his hands after using the toilet and all clients should be encouraged to do this.

Once functional independence has been achieved, clients can usually maintain their daily continence quite easily. Some may prefer to toilet themselves regularly, while others may prefer to toilet themselves according to need. Nocturnal continence may take longer to achieve.

3. MANAGEMENT OF MENSTRUATION

Coping with menstruation can create problems, particularly with less able clients. It can be stressful, or even frightening for those who do not understand the reason for menstrual bleeding, and in certain cases where clients react badly to menstruation there may be valid reasons for suppressing it.

Clients who have achieved some independence in toileting and personal hygiene routines should be able to learn to cope with menstruation, but training programmes are made considerably more difficult by (a) training opportunities only being available for 3–4 days per month, and (b) training occurring during a time when clients may suffer from premenstrual tension, lethargy, pain, and water retention.

Any training in this area should include some teaching about the reasons for menstruation. This will vary in complexity for each client, but everyone should understand that menstruation is a normal bodily function. Similarly, older women should understand that menstruation will eventually stop, and that this again is perfectly normal. The type of sanitary protection used depends entirely on the client and her personal preferences. However, less able clients are likely to find sanitary towels easier to cope with, at least initially, than tampons. Forward chaining is suitable for teaching functional skills, because dependence is reduced even if the whole teaching process is never completed, e.g. even if the client only learns to seek help at the onset of menstruation, or when towels/tampons need changing, they still have more control over their daily needs than previously.

Once the client has learned how to use and change her sanitary towels/tampons, she needs to be able to decide when towels/tampons need changing, and how to dispose of used items. The approach to teaching in this area is very similar to that used in toilet training, and there may be advantages, in view of the limited teaching time available, to initially teach the client to change her sanitary towel/tampon every time she uses the toilet. Disposal presents no problems because used towels/tampons can usually be flushed away and therefore existing toileting skills can be used.

4. WASHING

Skills needed for washing independence are recognition of body parts and the ability to sequence washing over the whole body. Bathing is the most difficult area to achieve true independence in, whereas strip washes or showers are easier to carry out (and have fewer safety problems). It may be better to teach a client to shower/strip wash independently (and so allow them more privacy), than to persist in teaching bathing, if a client will always need supervision. People who have continence problems may also develop dry skin through frequent bathing, so strip washing/showering is often more convenient and comfortable for clients.

As with many other self-care activities, washing is most effectively taught using a combination of chaining and prompting. Backward chaining is the technique of choice because it reinforces previous learning, and is less disruptive of the whole washing process. However, there may be occasions when it is preferable to prompt the entire task and then reduce the level of prompting given. Reinforcers (apart from verbal praise) can be difficult to incorporate into a washing programme, unless they are naturally linked with the activity, e.g. bubble bath, the use of shower gel rather than soap, or the use of a powder puff to apply talcum powder.

One of the commonest causes of failure in training is teaching the task too quickly, or teaching too much at once. Given the complexity of the task, it is far better to make each learning step too small and progress quickly through each stage to the end goal, than for each teaching step to take months to achieve. A well-structured programme should begin to show results in 3–4 weeks; if this does not happen, then check:

(a) the size of each teaching step,
(b) the type of reinforcement and reinforcers,
(c) the accuracy with which the programme is being administered.

5. HAIRWASHING AND STYLING

Hairwashing and styling requires a combination of physical skills, the ability to use a mirror and various tools, and an understanding of basic grooming procedures might ultimately only be mastered by the most able clients. Initially, teach each client to brush and comb her hair into a neat style, using prompting or if necessary prompting and chaining. A good cut is essential as it reduces the amount of effort and skill required to reproduce good results.

Teaching a client to wash and dry his/her hair is more complicated. Both require competence in visual perception and co-ordination, and are best taught by chaining. Whether to teach hairwashing first or last in the chaining process depends on each client, but as in all chaining processes, reinforcement at the end of the task is important. If hairwashing is being taught first, a simple cut or a permed style, which can be washed, towelled dry and combed into place, is helpful because the client, although learning only part of the whole skill, will see the finished hairstyle more quickly and need much less staff help.

Hairdrying needs to be taught systematically, using the same principles as hairwashing. Choose a cut that is easy to style, i.e. one that needs little blow-drying or curling, and then progress from styles that are virtually left to dry, to those which require more skill and precision. Gels and mousses also help a great deal. Once hairwashing and drying have been learned, clients should be taught hair care, i.e. what type of shampoo and/or conditioner to use, how frequently hair needs washing, how often hair needs cutting. Clients may take longer to achieve independence in these areas than in the more functional aspects of hairwashing and drying.

6. TOOTHBRUSHING AND DENTURE CARE

Toothbrushing is made up of four separate subsections:

(a) applying toothpaste,
(b) cleaning teeth,

(c) rinsing mouth,
(d) rinsing brush, and clearing away.

The whole task (a–d) is best taught in a backward chaining sequence, although each part may need to involve additional techniques. Electric toothbrushes can be useful, but may be offputting to some clients.

Applying toothpaste requires physical co-ordination, dexterity, precision and a conception of quantity. This skill can be taught using only chaining, but is more efficiently taught by involving prompting as well. Clients also need to learn how much toothpaste to apply to their brush, and automatic dispensers may help clients whose judgement of quantity and/or co-ordination is poor.

Cleaning the teeth is best taught as a whole sequence using verbal, gestural and physical prompts. Chaining is possible, but as the action takes place within the mouth, dividing the task into more than two or three parts is difficult in practice. It is better to begin by heavily prompting the entire task, and then gradually reduce the amount of prompting required until only verbal prompts are necessary. Rinsing the mouth is not readily prompted by encouraging the client to take a mouthful of water, as the natural reaction is to swallow the water. Consequently, modelling is best used here, so that the client can watch and copy appropriate actions.

For rinsing the brush and clearing away items used, backward chaining is again the best teaching technique to use. If this section is being taught in isolation from the other three then it would be possible to use forward chaining because of the variety of different actions included within the teaching step, but if backward chaining is the basis of the whole teaching programme, then it would be difficult to include a forward chaining element within it.

Denture wearers have slightly different problems, but the main approach to teaching is the same as above. The main difference is that clients need to be taught how to care for their dentures, and how to keep their mouth fresh and healthy. The most important factor in working with clients who wear dentures is to ensure that the dentures fit well. Dentures that irritate or rub the gums, or are loose-fitting or are unpleasant and/or painful to wear, may make clients resistant to any denture care training programmes.

7. SHAVING

The most obvious solution to shaving is growing a beard, because although it needs regular trimming, beard care is less onerous than shaving. But, if clients prefer to be clean-shaven then they need to select the method that is going to be most successful for them. An electric shaver is the easiest method to use as shavers can be used without a mirror (i.e. clients can learn to shave by touch rather than sight), and less precision is needed. Shaving with an electric shaver also has similarities to face washing, and the pre-training skills needed are therefore very similar.

Wet shaving is less similar to face washing, requires greater precision and visual awareness, and therefore may require a more lengthy teaching process. In both types of shaving, though, modelling is an appropriate technique to use initially, using chaining at a later stage to teach the more difficult aspects of the task.

8. APPEARANCE AND GROOMING

Care of appearance requires a variety of functional skills such as the application of make-up, selecting a personal style and keeping clothes in good order. Much of the work is based on self-image, so clients must be able to work with mirrors, and make appropriate allowances for the reversed image, before beginning appearance training.

Practically, a lot of appearance training is carried out informally in other areas of self-care activity, e.g. washing and dressing. Similarly, clients will hopefully formulate general ideas of appropriate appearance by following a dressing/clothes care programme. Much of appearance training, therefore, supplements current or previous teaching in other areas. Other aspects of training involve the acquisition of new skills, e.g. applying make-up. Most of these new skills are made up of ordered sequences and are therefore most suitably taught with a combination of backward chaining and prompting. However, modelling is also useful for clients who find it easier to copy actions than follow verbal instructions. It is also important to reinforce training by (a) informal modelling of appropriate appearance and good grooming by staff, (b) giving positive feedback and praise for each achievement, and (c) complimenting clients on their overall appearance.

9. EATING AND DRINKING

The skills involved in eating and drinking, as opposed to feeding and being fed, require more precision and dexterity, and may involve achieving certain standards of performance. Developing skill in eating and drinking is reinforcing to most clients, so motivation to learn is usually not a problem! Although in certain clients it may be necessary to prompt and facilitate feeding, functional problems associated with this area are usually caused by:

(a) general developmental delay;
(b) physical and neuromuscular disability, e.g. spasticity;
(c) abnormal reflex activity;
(d) impaired sensory, perceptual and visual ability.

When teaching clients to eat and drink independently, the usual approach of breaking the task down into its component parts and teaching those parts in an ordered sequence can be followed. For example, the analysis of eating using a spoon may include:

(1) grasping the spoon,
(2) putting the spoon into a dish or onto a plate,
(3) loading the spoon with food,
(4) bringing the spoon to within 6 inches (15 cm) of the mouth,
(5) bringing the spoon to within 2 inches (5 cm) of the mouth,
(6) putting the spoon into the mouth,
(7) removing the food from the spoon with the lips,
(8) removing the spoon to 2 inches (5 cm) away from the mouth,
(9) removing the spoon to 6 inches (15 cm) away from the mouth,
(10) returning the spoon to the plate.

This analysis is only an example. In reality the use of a spoon may need to be divided into many more detailed (or indeed less detailed) steps, according to each client's needs and abilities, and a wide variety of teaching techniques can be used to teach individual steps from the original analyses. Most teaching techniques begin by sitting beside the client and guiding them through the step or task being taught, and as each step is learned the prompting and support is faded out until the client can perform the action independently.

Other problems with eating and drinking may be caused by disruptive behaviour rather than any functional difficulties. Problems could include throwing food into the floor, refusing to use knives/forks/spoons, or refusing to sit near any other clients. Many behavioural problems can appear similar to developmental delays, and although these problems affect the actual mechanics of eating and drinking independently, behavioural causes need to be excluded before implementing any training programme.

Behavioural problems which result in clients refusing to eat correctly are usually managed by controlling access to food. This means that food has to be (a) only available at mealtimes for a specified amount of time, and (b) temporarily withheld at mealtimes for each incidence of a problem behaviour. This approach can be very effective, but does need to be carried out under medical supervision.

Training suggestions — eating

The bite reflex can make spoon-feeding difficult, as anything that is inserted into the mouth is immediately bitten. However, the development of chewing inhibits this response, so anything that increases chewing should be encouraged. The gag reflex, which can occur on its own, or with tongue extension, is usually found in people with an abnormally high hard palate. Gagging can cause food to accumulate, leading to further gagging and even vomiting, so the client should be encouraged to chew each mouthful (physically prompting chewing if necessary) and then to swallow all the food. Tongue thrust prevents any food from moving to the back of the mouth for swallowing, and as the mouth is usually open, causes the food to be thrust out of the mouth. Tongue thrust can be avoided by placing the spoon on the front of the tongue, then gently pushing it downwards and backwards before releasing the food.

Weak lip muscles cause excessive dribbling and make it difficult to keep any food in the mouth, but muscle tone can be improved by dabbing the lips with a napkin or towel, in order to prompt the closure of the mouth. Hypersensitivity around the face and mouth can cause great disruption to feeding, for obvious reasons. Desensitise this area before eating by stroking and touching the face with hands or with textured materials (e.g. napkins), working from the edges of the face towards the mouth. If this is successful, encourage the client to carry out similar desensitising procedures before eating.

Clients with physical disabilities should be seated in the most functional position before eating (or drinking) anything, as a stable position enhances any training programme. Clients who are still dependent on others should have the amount of help they receive in spoon-feeding gradually reduced. Use a small spoon and keep it horizontal in the client's mouth, avoiding either lifting the spoon upwards to help the client remove food from the spoon, or dropping food from the spoon into the mouth. Encourage the client to move his upper lip downwards to remove the food from the bowl of the spoon. Positioning small amounts of food on alternate sides of the spoon will also encourage tongue mobility and chewing. Once the client can remove food from a spoon, encourage more positive chewing skills by gradually introducing more firmly textured food, so that ultimately the client can transfer to a solid food diet.

Once clients can tolerate a solid diet, encourage them to finger-feed small portions of food, and then to take bites from larger pieces of food, e.g. from a piece of apple or bread. When a client is ready to start using cutlery for eating, begin with a spoon, then progress to using a fork (for appropriate meals), then a fork with a knife as a 'pusher/stabiliser', and finally to using a knife, fork or spoon in the conventional manner. The change from unilateral feeding to bilateral feeding can take some time to achieve.

Training suggestions — drinking

Drinking is slightly different from eating, as clients are likely to have had experience of drinking from a cup of some sort for some time before independence training begins, whereas eating is made more complex by the repeated introduction of new pieces of cutlery. In transferring from dependency to independency, cups can be protected by a lid or cover, and changed from a two-handled cup to a conventional cup, or from a closed cup to an open cup, as the client progresses. If initially a lot of help is needed, stand behind (or to one side of) the client and gently cup his chin in one hand while helping him to support the cup with your other hand. Teach clients to use a straw or length of polythene tubing when drinking, to strengthen lip control and prevent tongue thrust. Straws with valve controls, which prevent liquid from draining back into the cup or glass can be useful in early stage of training.

Clients with no functional problems should be taught to acquire independent drinking skills using behavioural principles. This requires careful analysis, and training programmes may need to be more specific than those used in other areas. Drinking can be taught using chaining, but equally prompting the entire task followed by fading out support may also be successful. Modelling may occasionally be useful in the later stages of training, when the client is refining existing skills.

Shaping is a slow method of training, but can be useful for either profoundly handicapped clients, or for those who are not responding very well to conventional teaching techniques. It is successful because it makes use of existing skills that are similar in some way to the target behaviour. Usually spoon-feeding is seen as the most suitable starting point for training, because spoon-feeding and drinking involve similar actions. With spoon-feeding, for example, shaping would gradually change the appearance of a spoon, making it gradually more and more like a cup, e.g.:

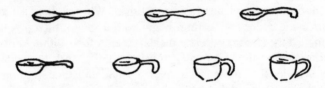

until a real cup could be substituted for the modified spoon.

SUMMARY

Intermediate living skills are, in some ways, the most difficult to teach of all living skills, because a high degree of change is required for the assimilation of new abilities and behaviours. With clients who are unlikely to progress further than this stage, training may be slow and difficult; for clients who are likely to be able to progress to advanced living skills, intermediate training needs to be thorough enough to provide firm foundations for future learning. In both cases the importance and difficulties of specific teaching in this level should not be underestimated.

References

1. M. Frostig *et al.*, *The Frostig Developmental Test of Visual Perception* (Follet Publishing Co., Chicago, 1966).
2. Toy Libraries Association, *The Good Toy Guide* (Toy Libraries Association, Potters Bar, Herts, 1982).

Further information

Perception/cognition

A.J. Ayres, *Sensory Integration and the Child* (Western Psychological Services, California, 1979).

A. Chappel *et al.*, *Developing Communication Skills* (Adult Literacy and Basic Skills Unit, London, 1983).

B.J. Cratty, *Perceptual and Motor Development in Infants and Children* (Prentice Hall, Englewood-Cliffs, New Jersey, 1979).

B. Vanwitsen, *Perceptual Training Activities Handbook* (Teachers College Press, New York, 1979).

S. Wolfendale and T. Bryans, *Identification of Learning Difficulties — a model for intervention* (National Association for Remedial Education, 1978).

Play

D. Jeffree and S. Cheseldine, *Let's Join In* (Souvenir Press, London, 1981).

D. Jeffree and R. McConkey, *Let's Make Toys* (Souvenir Press, London, 1981).

D. Jeffree *et al.*, *Let Me Play* (Souvenir Press, London, 1977).

R. Lear, *Play Helps* (Heinemann Medical, London, 1977).

J. and E. Newson, *Toys and Playthings in Development and Remediation* (Penguin, Harmondsworth, 1979).

B. Riddick, *Toys and Play for the Handicapped Child* (Croom Helm, London, 1982).

L. Rimmer, *Reality Orientation — principles and practice* (Winslow Press, 1982).

Toy Libraries Association, *The Good Toy Guide*, 1983.

Self-care

J. Carr, *Helping Your Handicapped Child* (Penguin, Harmondsworth, 1980).

D. Mandelstam (ed.), *Incontinence and its Management*, 2nd edn (Croom Helm, London and New York, 1986).

D.M. Millard, *Daily Living with a Handicapped Child* (Croom Helm, London and New York, 1984).

Other sources of intermediate living skills information can be found at the end of Chapter 5, Individual Teaching Programmes.

8

Developing Advanced Living Skills

Advanced living skill requires competence in a wide range of areas.

Advanced living skills are those which are needed to live safely and successfully within a community, or alone. These skills are not necessarily new ones, but higher and more specifically applied levels of intermediate skills. For example, work skills develop from play skills, and independent living skills develop from self-care skills.

The skills needed before advanced living skills training can begin are described in the previous two chapters, and without these skills training clients to live in the community is likely to be difficult. Additionally, although there is a very obvious division between different levels of independent living skills training within this book, in reality each client will probably be working on different levels of skills at the same time. It is likely that someone may be working on basic and intermediate skills concurrently, or intermediate and advanced skills concurrently, but less likely that someone undertaking advanced living skills training will still be working on developing basic living skills.

Some clients never reach this advanced stage of training, while others may achieve some skill in either one or two specific areas, or in the basic components of advanced living skills, but clients who do complete advanced living skills training have to experience (and cope with) a great deal of pressure in order to acquire the necessary coping abilities. To live successfully and independently requires mastery of work, domestic, academic and social skills, so this chapter concentrates on:

(1) Social and interaction skills,
(2) Literacy and numeracy skills,
(3) Community living skills,
(4) Work skills.

Training methods vary greatly in relation to each client and his work/living environment, but it is important to include as much practical experience as possible of meeting different people and situations. The ultimate aim of any advanced living training is to enable people to cope with solving difficulties, making decisions, taking action in a crisis/emergency and knowing how and where to obtain help where necessary.

SOCIAL AND INTERACTION SKILLS

The terms 'social skills' and 'interaction skills' are used in relation to the training needs of clients but their definitions can be confused, resulting in the phrases being used generically to describe any training. This leads to work, shopping or housework being included in social skills training, when these activities are the means through which social skills competence can be assessed, taught and practised. The differences between independent living skills, work skills and social skills are as follows:

(1) *Independent living skills* are the mechanical, practical and functional skills necessary to live safely, healthily and appropriately, without help or support.
(2) *Work skills* are the practical, cognitive and behavioural skills necessary to complete a task and/or maintain a job, to a standard suitable for employment.
(3) *Social and interaction skills* describe the perception, understanding and use of current social rules common to the local community, in order to maintain or develop relationships, acquire information and meet personal needs in all areas of life.

The development of all three types of skill usually takes place concurrently, but it is important to make a distinction between the teaching of social skills, and situations which allow social skills to be practised and applied. Most people acquire social skills throughout normal development by experience and by observation. Clients may find it difficult to learn about social roles and rules because of their limited social experience, restricted opportunities or because lower expectations lead to inappropriate behaviours being more readily tolerated in handicapped people. Lack of role experience is a real problem, and both training and living environments need to do all they can to provide as much diversity of role as possible. In normal development, a person progresses from being a child . . . to a pupil . . . to a student . . . to a girl/boyfriend . . . to a partner . . . to a parent . . . to a grand-parent, as well as taking on a wide range of other professional and social roles. The widest diversity of role that a client might experience is child/relative . . . to a pupil . . . to a trainee . . . to a friend. Drama, role play and creative media can be used in the training environment to encourage clients to experiment with different roles or to re-create family structures.

Communication is the medium usually used for social and interaction skills, and at the most basic level these skills are broken down into non-verbal communication, verbal communication and verbal/non-verbal interactions. Non-verbal communication is made up of facial signs and signals, physical posture, physical proximity, appearance, touch, tone of voice, gaze and gesture, and has three main functions:

(1) to complete or amplify the meaning of the spoken word by vocal emphasis, gesture and tone, thus increasing the overall comprehension of the message, and helping the listener to decide whether the speaker is being serious, amusing, sarcastic, etc.;
(2) to maintain interest, interaction and listener participation by voice modulation and cadencing, and by the use of various cues and mannerisms;
(3) to provide the speaker with feedback on the success of his communication, e.g. by maintaining eye contact, nodding or smiling.

Poor use of non-verbal communication gives the wrong feedback to people who are listening and interacting with the client, and the absence of, or inappropriate use of, cues and gestures is often the most noticeable thing that differentiates clients from other people in a social group.

Verbal communication is the basis of social interaction, although it relies on a wide range of non-verbal influences. There are various types of verbal communication:

(1) *Informal speech*, i.e. chatty, gossipy, jokey conversations which contain little actual information but nevertheless help to establish and develop relationships at all levels.
(2) *Personal speech*, i.e. speech which expresses and describes feelings, attitudes and emotions, and which provides real information about a client. This type of communication relies heavily on non-verbal input.
(3) *Performance speech*, i.e. communication which has a specific purpose. This type of speech is usually divided into two subtypes: (a) illocutions, where speech performs an action, such as voting or naming objects; and (b) perlocutions, where speech has a specific intention such as persuasion or intimidation.
(4) *Social speech*, i.e. standard phrases which ease interactions, such as greetings, apologies or thanks.
(5) *Latent speech*, where the actual information given is of secondary importance to the implied message, e.g. 'As I was saying to the Duke of . . .'. This type of speech is most commonly used to reinforce superiority or status.

The use and flexibility of verbal communication grows during normal development, and one of the many functions of play (in intermediate training) is to enable clients to try out different methods of communication.

Verbal and non-verbal interaction is the joint use of various types of communication. Most people learn, through experience, that using verbal and non-verbal communication concurrently is very effective, but to learn these skills clients require co-ordination and the ability to decide which type of interaction is best suited to each situation. Common types of interaction are:

(1) *Egocentric interaction*, i.e. talking about yourself with little regard for the participation of others. This is most usually found in young children.
(2) *Instructive interaction*, i.e. giving directions/instructions in order to influence the behaviour of others. This can range from being gently persuasive to firmly authoritarian.
(3) *Questioning interaction*, i.e. obtaining specific or general information in a direct or subtle form, using questions which are

open-ended or closed, impersonal or personal, intimidating or encouraging.
(4) *Informative interaction*, i.e. providing information in response to a given question, situation or discussion.

Eye contact is an important link for verbal and non-verbal interactions as, in a 1 : 1 interaction, 50 per cent of the time spent in looking, and a further 25 per cent of the time is spent in mutual gazing.[1] People who cannot produce this level of eye contact (quite apart from all other forms of non-verbal communication) give the impression of disinterest, dislike and dissatisfaction. Clients who cannot produce the correct level of eye contact are therefore handicapped *before* they even attempt any other form of interaction, so social skills training has to start at very basic levels.

Social skills training

Social skills training is basically a teaching process similar to those used to teach physical, behavioural and cognitive skills. The final level of ability will depend on each client's understanding, insight and potential for change, and on his present and future living environment. Any training will need to include:

conversation
understanding signs
understanding directions
decision-making
manners/politeness
making friends
use of non-verbal signs
use of gesture
understanding of non-verbal
  signs
listening skills
comprehension of verbal
  instructions
use of greetings and social
  speech
initiating interaction
recognition of mood in others

flexibility of role
achievement of goals
recognition of need in others
developing general rela-
  tionships
developing close relationships
asking questions
answering questions
reading
understanding social/
  community signs
recognising personal limitations
asking for relevant help
voice modulation and inflection
appropriate selection of
  clothing

logical and consequential
thought
appropriate social behaviour
making enquiries
comprehension of written signs
and instructions
maintaining relationships

giving and receiving non-
verbal feedback
maintaining interaction
concluding interactions
adaptability of approach
skill in formal interactions
developing friendships

This list includes only *some* of the necessary abilities for competency in advanced living skills. Successful acquisition of social skills needs not only specific teaching but also plenty of opportunities to practise and refine abilities. Social skills cannot be taught solely through individual or group work, but must also be backed up by working and living environments that demand the use of these newly acquired abilities. Consequently, social skills training relies heavily on the ideas of normalisation.

Staff modelling is very important, as there is little point teaching appropriate social skills if clients cannot see these skills being practised by those closest to them! The people who work with clients are the most valuable resource available; each client learns as much (if not more) from informal contact with relatives and carers as he does from formal teaching sessions, so the best possible use should be made of this medium. This means not only including 'please' and 'thank you' appropriately, but also demonstrating a full range of acceptable methods of interacting with others, emphasising the use of voice, non-verbal cues and gesture. Creative media, such as drama, can provide a much wider variety of social situations to experiment with, and can provide opportunities in which to practise skills before using community resources.

Practically, social skills teaching should start with basics, and consolidate the understanding and correct use of non-verbal signs, cues and gestures. Most psychiatric social skills groups are made up of people with a basic knowledge of non-verbal cues and gestures, who need help in applying this knowledge correctly, but no such assumptions can be made about clients on advanced training programmes. Much of the initial work is concerned with getting clients to look beyond themselves and relate positively to other people. This may involve defining the meaning of gestures and expressions (using videos and mirrors), and exercises such as looking at each other and describing appearance and mood, or trying to tell someone something by gesture and facial expression alone. It can be tempting to move rapidly on to more obviously useful social skills, such as those relating to dealing with certain situations, but while this can be done concurrently to maintain interest and variety, if the non-verbal stage of teaching is not given adequate attention, social competence will be difficult to achieve.

Social competence is the ability to gain desired effects or responses through communication and interaction. Social skills and interaction training are the means through which this competence can be achieved, and the key points of this training are:

(1) competence in the use of non-verbal signs and cues, together with varied use of the voice;
(2) responsiveness and the ability to feed back non-verbal reinforcement to the speaker;
(3) frequent practice and interaction with others of similar or higher levels of ability;
(4) physical appropriateness, e.g. dress, appearance, touch or posture;
(5) self-confidence and awareness of others.

Once some degree of competence has been achieved, the peer or social group in which a client lives and works becomes more important. At this point clients need social models with higher levels of ability than themselves, and this type of contact may only be possible outside the living and working environment. Social competence is different from other teaching goals in that the more proficient a client becomes, the less obvious their achievement is, i.e. appropriate behaviour is always less noticeable than inappropriate behaviour. However, reinforcement is no less necessary or welcome simply because advanced skills are being taught, and clients should always be given positive feedback on their progress.

LITERACY AND NUMERACY SKILLS

Literacy and numeracy are composite skills, i.e. literacy involves the ability to read, write and comprehend, while numeracy involves recognition and comprehension of number, capacity, weight, time and arithmetic, and many of these skills can be developed concurrently with communication skills. School-leavers and adults benefit from further training in literacy and numeracy, and non-teaching staff may find themselves involved in teaching these skills.

The information below gives various general ideas about how to develop skills in literacy and numeracy, but any specific difficulties should be referred to a teacher for help and advice.

Literacy

Many people never become truly literate, yet can still live successful and independent lives in the community. Literacy is certainly helpful, but a more crucial factor is access to help and support when necessary; if help is readily available when needed, then literacy is not essential. With clients who are unlikely to achieve full literacy, a great deal can still be done to develop recognition of social signs such as 'exit', 'toilet', and 'no entry', by shape, colour and association, and picture symbols in common use such as for 'women' and for 'men'. Clients may not be able to actually read these words, but they can identify patterns of letters or symbols with a particular meaning.

Clients who want to acquire high levels of literacy require sound perceptual skills, and need to have achieved mastery (during intermediate training) of pre-reading skills such as figure–ground discrimination, left–right tracking and hand–eye co-ordination, before they can begin training. Various adult literacy and special reading schemes are available, and teachers can advise on the best approach for each client. Many people, however, who are undertaking advanced living skills training, will already have some degree of literacy, and training needs to look at how their language and literacy skills are being used. The following skills may be involved:

Spoken language

clarity of articulation
use of prepositions
gives messages correctly
initiates conversation with
   friends
repeats a story correctly
describes items accurately
takes part in discussions
expresses feelings appropriately
gives information
   spontaneously
breadth of vocabulary
use of different tenses

reports on own experiences
initiates conversation with
   strangers
tells an imaginary story
   appropriately
gives directions accurately and
   clearly
reasons logically and
   appropriately
asks questions to obtain
   information
modifies level of voice
   appropriately

Listening skills

comprehends and reproduces information

listens and repeats information

listens and responds correctly to instructions

listens to and applies information gained

Writing skills

copies or traces letters

forms letters freehand

copies writing

writes spontaneously

writes words or names

writes simple sentences

writes letters

writes short stories or reports

writes imaginary stories

rewrites a story in own words

writes instructions for others

signs own name

Reading

knows key words and name

uses phonics to read new words

blends sounds to build words

understands simple sentences

deduces meanings of words from context

follows written instructions

reads newspapers and magazines

reads simple books

reads general books

reads for pleasure

uses library facilities

uses books for information

uses indexes

understands alphabetical order

interprets diagrams

knows commonly used words

General literacy needs to develop a broad, relevant vocabulary, which includes the use of synonyms and antonyms, e.g. big/large and big/small. Many creative activities can provide opportunities for developing this breadth of vocabulary.

Numeracy

Numeracy is involved in all aspects of daily life, and the understanding of number and quantity is more immediately important than reading and writing. Numeracy is found throughout self-care, work and social aspects of life, e.g. in the choice of quantity, use of money, and understanding of time. In daily life the minimum knowledge required is:

(1) an understanding of numbers 1–59, for time-telling;
(2) an understanding of numbers 1–100 for shopping and the use of money;
(3) an understanding of weight and fractions for cooking and shopping;
(4) an understanding of addition, subtraction, division and multiplication and the ability to complete simple mental arithmetic processes.

Again, specific advice relating to clients should be sought from teachers, but the information below may provide some ideas about the development of more general numeracy skills.

Sorting

Sorting exercises should emphasise aspects of quantity in daily life, using a wide range of words describing number and size, such as larger, shorter, longer, smaller, more, less, pound, ounces and grams. Sorting needs to be carried out to a high standard in advanced living training, and clients need to be able to make decisions about objects that do not precisely match any others.

Work sessions can require finished items to be sorted into boxes according to size, colour or shape; alternatively, creative sessions such as art/collage can involve clients in separating materials or subjects into similar types. Similarly, washing clothes provides a good opportunity for sorting items that need identical or different treatment.

Matching

Pairing and matching precedes more advanced number work, and opportunities for practising these skills can be included in most activities. Identification of pairs always precedes the interpretation of written symbols, and it is important that clients have sufficient skill in pairing before moving on to more advanced number work. For advanced living skills, abilities need to be developed to include the matching of signs and symbols to actual items, and eventually numerical signs such as $+$, $-$, $\times$, and $=$.

Counting

Most people have a good understanding of how to develop counting skills, but training should also include the use of cardinal and ordinal numbers, e.g. 6 cups/the 6th cup, 10 people/the 10th person. Games that require a running score to be kept are also useful in encouraging mental addition/subtraction.

Conservation of volume and number is related to counting, and can be encouraged by presenting equipment/materials in different ways and different containers. The ability to visually estimate the amount or number of items present is important, and staff should avoid always presenting information, materials or equipment in the same way.

Weight and capacity

An understanding of number and size is needed before concepts of weight and capacity can be acquired (often in conjunction with conservation of size and volume). Concept words such as full, half-full, empty, light/lightest, heavy/heaviest, balanced, equal, level, less than and greater than need to be learned.

Time

Time is a complex concept involving comprehension of time intervals (year, month, week, day), and position in time (tomorrow, today, yesterday, tonight, last week, next week), as well as time duration (second, minute, hour, day, week, fortnight) and the ability to identify any moment in time using a clock, watch and/or calendar. Verbal cues can help to form short-term time concepts, e.g. 'We're going shopping tomorrow morning, *after* you've had your breakfast', or 'We'll go home this evening, *after* it gets dark.' Long-term time concepts can be approached in a similar way, and can be illustrated by the use of activities such as horticulture, where changes can be matched to periods of time. Regular daily and weekly timetables can also help in the formation of time concepts, by allowing clients to match descriptive terminology to real events.

Learning to tell time usually starts with the recognition of hours, half-hours and quarter-hours, and then progress until time can be told to the precise minute. Finally the use of the 24-hour clock has to be learned. Time passage is learned in the same way, progressing from small time spans that are encountered daily to longer periods.

COMMUNITY LIVING SKILLS

Living completely independently is a highly complex skill which, in the normal course of development, is gradually acquired throughout childhood and adolescence. This process usually culminates with each individual leaving his parent's home to live a separate life.

Clients are often unable to follow this natural process because (a) their opportunities to acquire the relevant skills may be restricted and (b) there may be no facilities or resources available to allow clients to leave either their parental or residential home.

There is no easy way of giving a definitive list of the skills necessary for community living, but we have approached this training level by dividing competence into three broad, functional areas. The lists below give examples of *some* of the skills covered by each of these broad divisions, but they are by no means exhaustive. The main purpose of this section is to identify how broad and complex advanced living skills training needs to be. The three levels that make up community living skills are:

(1) *Personal skills.* Those skills which are necessary to establish and maintain a network of appropriate and meaningful relationships, interests and support systems — e.g. developing friendships, hobbies/leisure interests, travel and road safety, membership of clubs/libraries, correspondence, giving and receiving gifts, guests, social life, use of telephone and directories, sexual relationships and marriage.

(2) *Home management skills.* The technical and theoretical knowledge necessary to live safely, comfortably and healthily — e.g. housework, cooking, shopping, budgeting, use of banks and post offices, laundry and clothes care, nutrition, hygiene, health care, simple first aid, use of GP and dentist, care of pets, payment of bills, hire and rentals, home security and simple maintenance.

(3) *Self-reliance skills.* Those which are necessary for the individual to organise and maintain the resources they need — e.g. using community facilities, understanding contracts and rental/purchase agreements, understanding how and when to use emergency services, understanding the need for insurance, paying rent and organising holidays.

The remainder of this section looks in more detail at certain aspects of community living skills; departments or units implementing training at this level need to tailor their programmes both to the needs of the clients and the facilities available in the local community, e.g. local schools and colleges may have facilities and educational resources that can be tapped. As much training as possible should take place in the environment where it is going to be used.

Personal skills

Friendships

Individuals may need to be encouraged to develop friendships, and learn the skills required to do so. Obviously the development of friendships is likely to have been encouraged during earlier stages of training, but special emphasis may have to be placed at some point on involvement in clubs, social events and local recreational facilities. It is also important to encourage and teach clients to invite and welcome guests into their own homes. Too little attention to guests, and clients appear to be uninterested; whereas too much attention can be claustrophobic and unwelcome. The right and wrong ways to develop friendships, and react to guests, are usually observed through the family unit. The absence of a family unit makes learning these skills harder, and teaching may need to involve basic social skills as well as specific friendship skills.

Friendships can often be inhibited if no private space is available for conversation and shared activities. In residential units, there should be areas or rooms where clients can take their friends and visitors, and practise the skills that are being taught. Freedom to entertain also implies the need for clients to be able to visit their friends, so training needs to look closely at travel and the ability to orientate oneself to the community.

Hobbies/leisure interests

Training for community living should aim to provide each client with the ability to lead a full and satisfying life. Individuals with no hobbies/leisure interests (or no way of following their interests without help) can become isolated, and more restricted in their social contact. Leisure training needs to involve a wide range of experiences such as buying theatre/cinema tickets, buying a drink in a pub or using a swimming pool. Clients also have to understand a range of social signs and words such as 'exit' and 'entrance', and the symbolic signs for various activities. Special facilities are available through local and national sports agencies, but integration with local users is preferable.

Currently there is a tendency to minimise the amount of creative/craft media used in training, but creative media can be used constructively to develop interests into hobbies, and abilities into skills. The criteria for teaching an activity should always be the benefit and pleasure that each person gets from the activity, not the degree of skill likely to be achieved. However, dependence on other people can be frustrating, particularly if the help needed is minimal, e.g. being able to knit, but unable to cast off.

Travel and road safety

Training in this area should aim to ensure that anyone can confidently and safely follow regularly used routes, and obtain enough information to make unfamiliar journeys. Areas to be included are crossing the road, and the use of various types of transport (buses, trains, underground, taxis and, in certain instances, bicycles, boats and aeroplanes). Individuals need to be able to select the most appropriate method of transport, buy tickets, be able to find out departure times, and identify their destination. Travelling anywhere involves a degree of risk when a client travels alone for the first time. Backward chaining can help to overcome difficulties in recognising or remembering particular routes, but it is impossible to prepare for every eventuality.

Membership of clubs/libraries

Preparations for club membership may involve understanding of rules, payment of membership subscriptions, and making bookings. A lot of initial support and encouragement may be needed, and this should be as unobtrusive as possible. Libraries present a slightly different range of opportunities, but the training needs are the same. However, there may be more emphasis on the responsibilities of membership, e.g. punctual return of books, care of property and payment of fines.

Correspondence

Clients undertaking advanced training should know how to deal with letters, bills and other forms of correspondence. This does not necessarily mean that the client has to be able to read, but they should be able to take appropriate action, e.g. taking the letters to someone who can help, or acting on routine bills. On a more personal level, clients need to be able to summarise and exchange information.

Gifts

Part of the process of developing friendships and social contacts is the giving and receiving of gifts. Deciding who to give gifts or cards to may not be difficult (although some clients are rather indiscriminate in their gift-giving), but help may be needed in learning how to select and buy a suitable gift, or in how to receive a gift.

Giving gifts as a thank you gesture (e.g. after being invited for a meal) should also be included in this area of training.

Telephone

Using the telephone requires recognition of number, the ability to use a telephone directory or search through a list of numbers, to select and insert money (in a payphone), to dial a number and recognise tone codes, to talk to an unseen person and to take messages. Initially the use of the telephone can be practised in drama and social skills sessions, but learning to use a telephone independently has to involve real equipment. Reinforcement of the use of a telephone can be readily incorporated into training by encouraging clients to take and send their own messages.

Sexual relationships

The right to sexual relationships is still a subject that provokes heated discussion amongst staff and carers. Traditionally, it was felt that clients should be protected from sexual relationships, but current views support clients' right to express their sexuality in any way they wish. Obviously, there is still a need to protect vulnerable people from abuse, and to make services such as contraception available to those who want it, but many of the issues concerning the sexuality of people who happen to have a mental handicap are related to the prejudices and reactions of relatives, friends and staff, rather than the clients themselves.

Accepting that clients have the right to express their sexuality places certain demands on training and living environments. Firstly, each client must have access to privacy whenever needed; secondly, clients must be given the knowledge and information they need to make informed decisions about their sexual needs, and thirdly, they must learn how to express their needs within accepted social standards.

The whole question of sexual skills and behaviour is often avoided because staff either actively disagree with its discussion, or are embarrassed about including relevant teaching in the overall training programme. Any training must obviously be given sensitively and appropriately for each client. Ignoring sexual needs may be convenient for staff, but is hardly sensible in programmes training clients in community living skills.

Home management skills

Housework

Competence in keeping home and clothing clean is an important advanced living skill. The creative media used in intermediate training provides general experience of cleaning and tidying, but specific development of cleaning skills needs more individual input. It is usually initially easier to implement training in the client's bedroom, before moving on to more general household cleaning. Training can then progress by either applying the skills used in bedroom care to all rooms, or gradually learning how to clean and care for other rooms.

Any training should use modern equipment and materials to best advantage, e.g. using the easiest spray polishes, and teaching the quickest cleaning methods. There is no point in teaching excessively thorough cleaning methods, when the main aim of training is to ensure that someone is able to keep a home in a reasonably clean and tidy condition. Impossibly high standards defeat the object of the exercise.

Cooking

Cooking can also provoke strong feelings in staff and carers. Some people feel that it is essential that clients should be completely independent in this area, but with an increasing range of convenience meals and foods available this is no longer so. As long as someone is capable of selecting a balanced diet, the technical skills needed can be minimal, and in reality it may be more effective to place greater emphasis on understanding nutritional requirements, the selection and cooking of convenience foods, and the preparation of simple snacks and drinks. However, if clients are able to acquire some level of cooking ability, then traditional methods should be taught.

Time is often the factor which prevents true independence; clients may be able to cook a complete meal independently, but require 2–3 hours to do so. Speed comes with the ability to carry out several procedures and processes concurrently, e.g. making gravy while watching the main course cook, setting the table and preparing the vegetables. Clients may not have the confidence or ability to juggle work in this way, in which case the use of convenience foods (e.g. instant gravy or custard) may reduce the amount of overall time needed. Similarly, microwave ovens may reduce the overall meal preparation time, while still allowing clients enough time to confidently prepare the food. Generally, basic cooking still requires four separate abilities:

(1) familiarity with techniques, terminology, sequences and procedures;
(2) independence in producing a complete snack or meal (either from raw materials or from convenience foods);
(3) shopping and budgeting skills;
(4) an understanding of nutritional needs.

Traditional cooking methods, however, can be greatly simplified by modifying rules and procedures. This may limit the range and standard of ability slightly, but makes it easier for more people to acquire the basic skills. These modifications are:

(1) *Using large quantities* that are easier to weigh out and work with. It is easier to make enough for two meals than to weigh out fractions of an ounce.
(2) *Converting small measures*, e.g. ¼ ounce, into teaspoon equivalents. Weighing scales usually require small amounts to be weighed by visually estimating the position of a spring-loaded pointer between two points and it is easier and more accurate to measure these small amounts as two or three teaspoons. Liquid measures of less than ¼ pint should also be converted in this way.
(3) *Using balance scales* rather than spring-loaded scales, as individual amounts are more clearly and accurately measured in the former. In spring-loaded scales each individual quantity has to be recognised on the display face or digital display, whereas once the correct weights have been chosen with balance scales, the same movement always indicates that the correct weight has been reached.
(4) *Simplifying cooking temperatures* to low, medium and high. These temperatures may be gauged by the position of any control switch, i.e. low is immediately after turning on, medium is half-way between the lowest and highest temperatures, and high is as far as the switch will turn. Having only three temperatures simplifies cooking procedures considerably, i.e. low temperatures are used for warming pre-cooked food, medium temperatures are used for the majority of cooking procedures, and high temperatures are used only for fast types of cooking or boiling.

(5) *Standardising cooking times*, e.g. all vegetables are cooked for 15 minutes, all pies are cooked for 40 minutes, and all casseroles/stews are cooked for 90 minutes. Using standardised times means that some of the food may be slightly overcooked, but on balance most meals will be satisfactory.

(6) *Using the oven and grill* in preference to oven-top cooking, especially for fried foods. Food cooked in the oven is easier to manage than food spluttering in a frying pan; clients who like fried foods can always use frozen oven-cooked products, or visit their local fish and chip shop!

(7) *Using standardised basic recipes* which clients can then adapt in a variety of ways. A comprehensive diet can be cooked by varying just seven basic recipes or procedures (pastry, batter mixtures, sponge mixtures, sauces, casseroles/oven cooking, boiling and toasting) with sweet and savoury ingredients.

(8) *Using convenience foods* wherever possible, along with labour-saving equipment such as food mixers/food processors.

(9) *Reducing each process to a minimum number of steps*, or using an all-in-one method. For example, a flan recipe which requires certain ingredients to be fried before they are added can have this step omitted and the cooking time slightly lengthened. This makes little difference to the taste, but the simplified procedure is a great advantage.

Individuals who follow this method of learning to cook need recipe cards or books that give the details of the special or standardised recipes involved. However, over-dependence on written or pictorial recipes should be avoided. Clients may also need tuition in the short-hand or jargon associated with cooking, e.g. 'oz' for ounce, 'lb' for pound and 'tbsp/tsp' for tablespoon/teaspoon. Finally, independence in cooking can only really be acquired if the client has the opportunity to regularly practise these skills alone. Problems will inevitably arise, and clients must be able to cope with them on their own, and also be able to take responsibility for the risks involved.

Shopping

Shopping requires a range of discriminatory and perceptual abilities, e.g.:

(1) the identification of needs in terms of quantity, size, weight, shape, colour, quality;

(2) the identification and selection of the best place to find the items

143

wanted, e.g. local shops, department stores, discount houses, mail order catalogues;
(3) the selection of the most appropriate items according to likes, values and means;
(4) the understanding and use of various forms of payment such as cash, cheques, credit cards;
(5) the understanding of payment and collection procedures.

Before any training is implemented the client needs to be able to select items according to brand names, clothing sizes, etc. Practical training is best managed using a chaining process until the client can complete the entire process alone. Shopping training should include not only the use of a variety of different types of shops, but also needs to include use of transport, and equipment such as escalators and lifts.

Budgeting

Budgeting needs to take place in conjunction with other home management skills. To be independent, a client needs to know:

(1) how much their income is per day/week/month,
(2) what needs to be bought each day/week/month,
(3) how much money needs to be saved each day/week/month for long-term goals (e.g. holidays),
(4) how much money is left for personal spending after (2) and (3) have been deducted from (1).

It is also necessary for each client to have some conception of simple economies, e.g. choosing fresh foods that are in season and therefore cheaper, or choosing chain-store makes rather than brand names. This requires an understanding of arithmetical procedures, the ability to compare relative values and the ability to make value judgements about the cost of several items. Budgeting also implies a need for money management, and clients need to learn about methods by keeping money, including how to use banks and post offices.

Nutrition

Anyone learning to care for himself must learn something of nutrition, in order to maintain a healthy diet. The easiest way to teach basic nutrition is to use a simplified approach similar to that used in cooking. In such a system clients learn to divide foods up into different types according to their *main* constituents, e.g. milk, cheese and meat are all proteins, butter and cream are fats, jams and sauces are sugars, bread and cakes are starches, and vegetables and fruits are vitamins. Individuals can then plan meals that contain something from each category, and more protein and vitamins than sugars, starches and fats. This type of simplified system pays no attention to fibre, trace elements or minerals, but generally it should ensure a reasonably balanced diet.

Laundry and clothes care

Laundry and clothes care involves ability in five different areas:

(1) handwashing,
(2) use of spin dryers and tumble dryers,
(3) machine washing (twin tub or automatic),
(4) use of launderette facilities,
(5) airing and ironing.

At the simplest level all items can be handwashed, but this is time-consuming and tiring. Using machines gives each client more time to be spent of other aspects of home management. However, all training should be carried out at appropriate times of the day, and not as part of a work-orientated training programme. This area of training should also include shoe care, and simple repairs to clothing.

Hygiene

Hygiene is an important aspect of preventive care that needs to be included in training programmes. Poor hygiene affects not only health, but also social interaction and the development of good community relationships. It is not always necessary for clients to have a detailed knowledge about *why* different procedures should be followed, but they must be aware of the importance of certain hygiene routines. As in many advanced areas, foundation skills are acquired through intermediate activities, e.g. learning to wash hands after using the toilet, or before the preparation of food.

Health care

Clients need to be able to cope with minor health problems in their own home, and this includes basic first aid, i.e. taking pain-killers, cleaning wounds, applying plasters/bandages, using antiseptics or taking cough medicines. In addition, clients need to know when to

145

seek professional help or advice, such as in the case of continued pain, bleeding or discomfort. Most clients can take a much more active and responsible role in their own health care than they are allowed, although residential units often have safety guidelines that prevent clients from administering their own medication. However, there is still much that can be done outside these constraints to allow each client more responsibility.

Use of the doctor and dentist

Community living requires clients to be able to obtain medical and dental services independently. Training in this area can be started during intermediate/early advanced living training, by first learning how to make appointments via members of staff, then via the telephone, and finally to take complete responsibility for attending to medical and dental needs. Residential environments can be structured to help develop these skills; if all medical and dental services run as closely to the normal community practice systems as possible, then clients will automatically have opportunities to acquire the relevant skills.

Pet care

Part of home management may involve owning and caring for pets, and clients who like animals should be encouraged to choose a pet that is suitable to their lifestyle, environment and financial means. Clients then need to learn how to care for their animals, which may involve feeding, cleaning, exercising, general care, health care and holiday care. Clients need to be reliable and responsible in their attitude to pet ownership, and these qualities can easily be assessed in home and work environments.

Bills and rents

Unless costs are included in the amount charged for rent, clients will have to learn to pay for materials and/or services provided. Opportunities for payment can be included in intermediate and early advanced living skills training, but at some point each client needs to learn more specific bill-paying skills. This includes understanding different payment methods, e.g. paying by cash, by cheque or by standing order. Hire and rental agreements are different methods of bill-paying, and should also be included in a comprehensive training programme. Hire and rental companies vary in the freedom they extend to clients; some are quite happy to issue agreements to clients in their own right, while others require staff to countersign any such agreement. Clients should have the right to take out their own rental agreements, but this issue may have to be sensitively handled at a local level.

Home security

The skills required to protect yourself and your property range from learning to operate and use keys and locks, to understanding which measures are necessary for home protection, e.g. window locks, door bolts and safety chains. This implies a need for clients to understand *why* these measures are necessary, and it may therefore be necessary also to teach basic aspects of self-defence and self-protection, e.g. avoiding dimly lit or lonely short cuts, carrying the minimum amount of cash, or checking the identification of workmen visiting the home.

Self-reliance skills

Community facilities

Each community has a range of public facilities which can be used for work, personal or social purposes. Clients often have limited experience and understanding of the services and resources available, and may not have a social circle which is wide enough to gather that information informally. Training therefore needs to give each person a thorough orientation to the local community, and enable clients to both understand and use the range of opportunities and services available to them.

Contracts and work agreements

Anyone living in the community who has a job, or attends a work centre, needs to understand contractual obligations. This can vary from understanding the importance of punctuality, appearance and attitude to work, to understanding pay scales, gradings, sick leave and holiday procedures and trade union rights. Many details can be simplified, while others can be best explained by simulating work conditions within the training programme.

Emergency services

Clients living in the community need to know how to obtain help in cases of personal or general difficulty, or in response to a crisis. All clients need to know how to summon fire, ambulance or police services, and to understand what these services are to be used for.

Insurance and legal issues

Clients who acquire their own possessions should understand enough about insurance policies to be able to make an informed decision about whether or not they wish to insure their belongings. Clients also need to understand their basic legal rights. This is best approached by initially outlining fundamental rights, and then expanding on this whenever relevant situations occur. One right that clients may need to be encouraged to exercise is the right to vote. Clients often have no experience of voting, and training needs to include information about the reasons for voting, the issues involved, and the procedures involved in voting.

Directories

In all aspects of daily life, information is taken from lists, timetables, directories or indexes. Individuals who are literate can become much more self-reliant if they are able to extract information from these sources, rather than having to ask others for help. Scanning lists and directories is an advanced skill, and not all clients will learn to do this, but those that are able should be actively encouraged to do so.

Living in the community requires the co-ordination of a vast array of individual skills which, in normal development, are acquired over approximately the first 20 years of life. Clients have to go through the same processes, but are often under pressure to learn the same skills in considerably less time. Key aspects in developing community living skills are:

(1) creating an environment which actively encourages independence in every aspect of daily life;
(2) differentiating between *essential* and *useful* skills, or levels of ability;
(3) simplifying or standardising training so that general rules can be learned and applied;
(4) tailoring training to meet the needs of the client and his future home.

The criterion for success should ultimately be the ease with which each client is able to integrate into the local community, not the degree of skill acquired in any given area.

WORK SKILLS

The United Nations Declaration on the Rights of Mentally Retarded Persons (1971) said:

> The mentally retarded person has a right to economic security and to a decent standard of living. He has the right to perform productive work or to engage in any other meaningful occupation, to the fullest possible extent of his capabilities.

Declarations of rights, however, do not assure clients of jobs or productive work. Individuals may be appropriately skilled, reliable and able to live independently in the community, but still remain within training centres because (like many other people) they cannot find work. Sheltered work schemes, where clients are employed to produce goods for sale, are one answer. Traditionally these schemes have used industrial work, but horticulture and furniture-making are also being used. Unless these schemes are backed by charities or other funding, the work must be self-financing through sales. Apart from the difficulties of finding work, the most common reasons for failure are:

(1) prejudices against people who have a mental handicap;
(2) over-protection by relatives, staff and possibly employers;
(3) inability to travel independently;
(4) rushed or superficial work training;
(5) poor pre-employment training;
(6) inappropriate placement at work;
(7) poor support and training in the initial stages of employment.

Work and work training meet two different needs. Work sessions use existing skills in the production of various saleable items, and can be very valuable in maintaining the self-esteem of those who, if more jobs were available, would be able to work in the community. Work training, however, is a medium through which work-related skills such as punctuality, concentration, persistence and stamina are developed; the actual task is relatively unimportant in relation to the development of desirable attributes. The criterion for success in work sessions is an increased level of production and quality; the criterion for success in work training sessions is the development of individual abilities. Both uses of work, though, rely on a constant supply of constructional and organisational work.

Much of advanced living skills training, however, assumes that clients will work, and if this is not a realistic goal then work training must be critically reviewed in order to ensure that its inclusion in a training timetable is valid.

Work training

Developing competent work skills is a lengthy process, involving not only vocational skills, but also self-help, social and academic skills. To work successfully a client must be able to:

(1) attend to his individual needs;
(2) get on well with colleagues and supervisors, and understand the importance of good social relationships;
(3) read and understand enough to cope with the verbal, written and diagrammatic aspects of a job;
(4) physically perform any task (either with or without training) to desired standards.

The proportional importance of each of these skill areas depends on the type of job and work environment, and work training should aim to either simulate the demands of an envisaged work environment, or teach clients flexibility of approach. For example, therapeutically orientated staff may see competence in social and self-help skills as the most important areas of work, on the assumption that if general work habits are good the actual work task can be readily learned. Employers, on the other hand, may place more importance on high levels of production or accuracy than on social/self-help skills.

Training should be as realistic as possible, even to the extent of creating likely pressures and conflicts within a training group. Some of the skills clients should acquire are:

speed	consistency
responsibility	adaptability
adaptability to environment	acceptance of supervision
high work quality	accuracy
self-checking of work	good concentration
care of tools/equipment	good communication
adequate memory	regularity of attendance
comprehension of instructions	reliability
self-confidence	decision-making

adequate personal hygiene
good relationships with
   colleagues
ability to cope with pressure

foresight and initiative
punctuality
perseverance

Work training groups should also provide the opportunity to deal with changing tasks and circumstances, and teach clients about pay, deductions, rights and contracts.

Work groups

Work groups aim to provide clients who are, unable to find employment with the chance to participate in the production of saleable items. Work groups can also provide some income for members of the group, particularly if the standard of the finished articles is high. Some of the principles of work training apply to work groups, although less specifically and with less urgency; the most important being that work groups should run for the benefit of the group members, and not need the group members solely for their ability to produce saleable goods.

Provision of work

There are four main methods of providing work:

(1) contract work with a local supplier;
(2) production of own-design items for sale;
(3) provision of services, e.g. collating of blank papers for case note files;
(4) production of non-saleable items or services for others, e.g. making toys for children.

(1) *Contract work* is mainly made up of simple constructional tasks. Some of the work is dirty, fiddly and poorly paid, and as there are usually weekly quotas to meet, this type of work takes a lot of staff time and needs a work force who can consistently work on a given job. The low pay rates also mean that workers cannot be adequately paid for their work.
(2) *Making and selling original designs* is a much better option. The production of work is controlled by the work group, and as all

151

the money from sales returns to the group, clients have a better opportunity to receive a realistic wage for their work. However, items produced still need to be of a high standard in order to ensure that enough can be sold to maintain income. Gardening work is a varied and useful activity, providing constant work and producing very saleable items. Raising money or producing articles for other groups of people can also be seen as appropriate activities for work groups. Ideas for work products can be gleaned from a variety of sources and adapted to suit particular needs; additional ideas for work projects can be found in Chapter 10, Group Work Activity Ideas. Presenting products in a professional way is important, and also provides more work tasks. Simply packing cards in plastic bags and sealing them with printed self-adhesive labels can do a great deal to improve the product's saleability.

(3) *Provision of services for others* can be a useful source of work, as long as both parties benefit from the arrangement. Traditionally jobs such as assembling empty case note files, or packing sterile supplies for operating theatres, have been used, but staff have to be careful that undertaking these jobs is not compromising the value of their clients. Some work projects, e.g. writing and producing a monthly newsletter, provide a service to both clients and associated people alike, and these types of projects may be preferable.

(4) *Production of non-saleable items for others* can also be valuable in work sessions, and help each client to identify with his local community/environment. Tasks such as preparing for forthcoming events, making toys for handicapped children, or raising money for a Christmas outing for everyone, can all be used to either provide work or train work skills. Using this type of activity also involves each client in his environment, and helps build up appropriate relationships.

Payment for work

This is an issue within work training for which there is no right or wrong answer, although there is a danger that payment can blur the therapeutic reasons for providing work. As a general guide, though, if less than 50 per cent of a weekly training timetable is given over to work-related activities then it is probably better to avoid paying group members; in this type of situation members can develop their own hierarchies of preferred group, and want to attend only those that are the most profitable. This inevitably discriminates against the less able, and it is therefore better to encourage attendance at work groups through other means.

However, if advanced living skills training has reached the stage where it is desirable to simulate a work environment, then this will necessarily involve a larger percentage of work-related activities, and payment then becomes a useful means of training. Payment in these instances underlines the link between quality and quantity of work, and income. Balancing the payment at an appropriate level is more difficult, though. Payment should provide sufficient incentive to motivate clients to work, but should also be less than the amount each client would be likely to receive from a job or alternative training placement. This is easy if a client is likely to move on to an ordinary job, as all jobs are likely to be paid more than a training unit, but sheltered work places or training centres have much lower pay levels, and consequently work training pay may need to be lower than this in order to maintain motivation for certain clients. Pay is also usually limited by income from sales!

SUMMARY

Advanced training is made up of a broad range of training areas, yet requires clients to develop very specific knowledge within those areas. In addition to this huge load of learning, clients have to acquire these new skills and abilities very quickly. Consequently, the only realistic way to approach advanced living skills training is to prioritise skills areas in relation to the client's envisaged living environment and local community, and to make sure that these skills are thoroughly learned. The most usual prioritisation is to teach skills affecting personal relationships first, work- and home-related skills second and self-reliance skills last.

Reference

1. M. Argyle and M. Cook, *Gaze and Mutual Gaze* (Cambridge University Press, Cambridge, 1976).

Further information

Social skills

M. Argyle, *The Psychology of Interpersonal Behaviour* (Penguin, Harmondsworth, 1985).

M. Argyle, *Social Interaction* (Tavistock Publications, London and New York, 1973).

R. Ellis and D. Whittington, *A Guide to Social Skill Training* (Croom Helm, London/Brookline Books, Cambridge, Massachusetts, 1981).

P. Williams and B. Shoultz, *We Can Speak for Ourselves* (Souvenir Press, London, 1982).

Literacy and numeracy skills

D. Jeffree and M. Skeffington, *Let Me Read* (Souvenir Press, London, 1980).

J. Thatcher, *Teaching Reading to Mentally Handicapped Children* (Croom Helm, London and New York, 1984).

The following learning sets may also be useful:

GOAL (Game Orientated Activities for Learning), developed by Dr Merle B. Kanes from LDA, Aware House, Duke Street, Wisbech, Cambs.

Community living skills

M. and A. Craft, *Sex and the Mentally Handicapped* (Routledge & Kegan Paul, London and New York, 1982).

R. Grice, *A Life of Your Own — project books* (Cassell, London, 1975).

A. Hanson, *Ready to Leave — project books* (Collins, London, 1979).

R.M. Marshall, *My Cookbook* (British Institute of Mental Handicap, Worcestershire, 1983).

R. Meyers, *Like Normal People* (Souvenir Press, London, 1979).

E. Whelan and B. Speake, *Learning to Cope* (Souvenir Press, London, 1978).

Work skills

Employment Services Agency, *Employing Someone who is Mentally Handicapped* (leaflet, 1976).

D. Hutchinson, *Work Preparation for the Mentally Handicapped* (Croom Helm, London, 1982).

H. Schlesinger and E. Whelan, *Industry and Effort — a study of work centres in England, Wales and Northern Ireland* (Heinemann Medical, London, 1979).

E. Whelan and B. Speake, *Getting to Work* (Souvenir Press, London, 1981).

9

Planning Group Work

Therapeutic group work has to be carefully structured to meet everyone's needs.

While any training related to personal skills — e.g. washing, dressing, feeding, counting or reading — should first be taught individually and then consolidated within activity groups, any skills requiring interaction, co-operation or sharing are best taught within a group (no matter how small) where feedback on performance is available from other group members. This type of therapeutic work group has three aims:

(1) to encourage and develop each client's abilities within a given area of function, e.g. increasing concentration span, stamina, tolerance of pressure, communication skill or problem-solving ability;
(2) to provide general training activities (holding activities) from which people with particular needs can be withdrawn for specific individual work;
(3) to provide opportunities for experimenting with social roles and behaviours in a supportive environment.

Running therapeutic groups requires a skilful approach and a clear understanding both of the needs of the group and the needs of each individual within the group. Very often groups achieve their aims through the use of creative media, but staff must be able to distinguish between a creative activity used recreationally and one

Figure 9.1: The group process

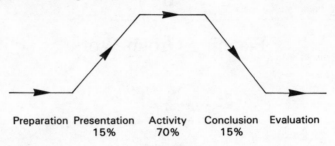

Preparation Presentation   Activity   Conclusion   Evaluation
15%   70%   15%

In a 1-hour group this would give approximately 10 minutes to presentation, 40 minutes to the planned activity and 10 minutes to the conclusion.

which is used therapeutically. For example, a cooking session can be used to make cakes to eat, or it can be used for conceptual work, practice in dexterity, manipulation, hand–eye co-ordination, comprehension and/or sensory stimulation. Anyone involved in providing therapeutic group work should be able to provide aims/objectives for the training sessions they run.

Aims and objectives provide statements about what each group is trying to achieve, but the staff running each group have to interpret these aims and objectives into sessional training plans. This means staff have to select certain aspects of the overall goals, and then form them into a plan of work for the individuals within the group. At this point, although the direction of training and type of media used are known, there is still much that can be done to shape the success (or otherwise) of the group. There are three broad areas of influence:

(1) the structure used to run a group,
(2) the manipulation of the teaching environment,
(3) the use of role and personality.

RUNNING GROUPS

The content and duration of a group activity varies in relation to the ability level of the group members, the creative medium used, and the staff : client ratio. Common to all training activities, though, is the group structure. Running a group can be divided into five distinct

156

parts: preparation, presentation, activity, conclusion and evaluation. The basic sequence is shown in Figure 9.1.

Preparation

Preparation should, in effect, be the procedure for getting everything (e.g. materials, visual aids, equipment, etc.) ready at the right time, and in the right place. Preparation also includes the formulation of teaching objectives and session plans. Teaching objectives should be formally written down for reference, but sessional plans only need to be brief notes about the order of work, and activities to be used. The more experienced staff become, the briefer these preparatory notes can be, but plans should never be so inflexible that they cannot incorporate spontaneous developments into the session. If more than one person is running a training group, then written objectives and shared sessional planning are essential. Once short-term/teaching/sessional objectives have been decided, the following points should also be considered:

(1) If a creative medium is being used, which are the most effective aspects of that medium for your purposes?
(2) Does any part of the activity and/or creative medium have any implications for special safety or health precautions?
(3) Will the training group be made up of one major activity, or several smaller, interrelated activities, and if so, how are these subsections to be related and presented?
(4) Does any part of the activity require the group to be subdivided, and if so, how will this be done?
(5) What differences are there in sex, age, ability range, behaviour, motivation and concentration amongst group members, and how does this affect the session plan?
(6) Do any group members have additional management programmes or teaching objectives that have to be incorporated into the session, and if so how will this be managed?
(7) How can the available staff be used to best advantage?
(8) Is the environment suitable for the activity, and if not, what changes can be made?
(9) What equipment and materials are needed for the activity, and are they available?
(10) What will be the running order of the group, and who will do what?

157

Presentation

This is the time when the staff within a group prepare the group members for the activity. This may involve positioning clients, explaining what is required, or setting goals. The result of this part of the activity should be clients who are motivated to work well, and who understand what is going to happen. Stimulation of interest and motivation can be achieved by:

(1) showing examples of what is to be produced, or achieved;
(2) giving a verbal description of what is going to happen, e.g. identifying the ingredients and processes involved in baking;
(3) asking group members to describe themselves, their colleagues or any recent news/events;
(4) stretching and limbering-up exercises, or massage;
(5) discussion about themes or general topics, before investigating them further, e.g. discussing what everyone is wearing before looking more closely at descriptive words and concepts associated with appearance and self-care.

Presentation and motivation should not be hurried, and may require instructions, descriptions and concepts to be repeated until understood. Staff should be able to present the same information and instructions in a variety of ways, to ensure that everyone understands and is ready to participate in the activity.

Activity

This is the part of the group session when the clients work through the session plan and try to meet the objectives that have been set. If the session has been subdivided, then the various subsections should link together to form a cohesive whole. For example, in a keep-fit session, the links between subsections could be:

warming-up exercises . . . movement around the room, ending in each client picking up a hoop . . . using the hoops for balance and floor exercises . . . working in pairs using hoops . . . races to put the hoops away . . . relaxation.

Initially, achieving fluent, smoothly run groups can be hard work, but skill comes with experience and attention to planning. Group members should be encouraged to contribute ideas and information that can be incorporated into the session, and consequently staff running groups need to be confident of their own ability to deal with these contributions and with problem situations. Confidence also comes from identifying what form potential problems are likely to take, and being prepared for them in advance.

One of the most common problems is running out of work, or finding that the work planned is either too easy or too hard for the group members. This latter problem can be avoided by discussing ideas for up-grading or simplifying different activities in the planning and preparation procedures, but when planned activities take less time than envisaged the solution depends on the type of medium that has been used. Music, drama and singing lend themselves to improvisation, and all these media are easy to extend to fill in the time available. In activities with a specific goal or end-product it is easier to extend to fill in the time available. In activities with a specific goal or end-product it is easier to extend the concluding section of the group rather than to try to add in more work. In task-orientated activities there are usually routine cleaning and tidying activities, and these can be made into learning situations to support the activity section. The best method, though, of dealing with running out of work is to over-plan the content of the activity. For example, if an hour-long session is to include teaching on six separate subjects, then prepare 50 per cent more work than is likely to be needed, i.e. nine teaching areas. If the 'activity' time within an hour-long group is only 40 minutes, then this gives each teaching subject less than 5 minutes, and it is unlikely that groups of four or more clients will complete each activity in less than 5 minutes. Individual teaching areas that are not needed can be deferred for use in subsequent sessions.

Poor participation and support from helpers in the group usually indicates either lack of involvement in planning and preparation, or lack of understanding, e.g. in how to use equipment, or manage problem behaviours. It could also be a symptom of the boredom of both staff and group members, and the solution to both reasons is obvious! A more difficult staff problem to solve is where someone is unaware that his style of participation is inappropriate, or conflicts with recognised objectives, e.g. refusing to join in, over-participating, talking throughout teaching/instructions or making fun of clients. Some response must be made to this type of problem, but it must be sensitively managed. It is inappropriate to draw attention to the problem in front of group members, yet the problem has to be solved quickly in order to avoid compromising teaching objectives. The problem could possibly be abstractly dealt with by using the planning time to discuss the sorts of behaviours staff are to model, but if this does not work the problem must be confronted and solutions worked out.

Less frequently, situations can occur when staff are absent, or emergencies occur that take staff away from the group for a period of time. Given sufficient forewarning, some sessions can be combined to pool available staff, but if this problem occurs during a group session then there is little choice but either to carry on with the planned activity or to substitute an alternative activity. There is no easy answer to this, but developing an activity that can be quickly and easily run with the minimum number of staff, e.g. a singing session, can be very helpful.

Conclusions

Like the presentation, the conclusion of the group session should relate to the actual teaching content, although whereas the presentation interests, prepares and motivates group members to the work, the conclusion provides reinforcement for achievement, feedback on performance and consolidation of key training issues. Successful conclusions should leave the group members feeling proud of their achievements, and happy to participate in the activity again. Examples of ways to conclude a group are:

(1) looking at each person's finished work, comparing it to the original example, and restating the materials and processes that were used to create it — this can be followed by displaying the finished work, if appropriate;
(2) reviewing individual performance or the amount of progress that has been made with a project;
(3) combining various social or interaction skills into linked actions or demonstrations, and discussing how these might be practised;
(4) using quiet relaxing activities after physically strenuous sessions;
(5) a resumé of the main conceptual teaching areas that have been worked on.

The conclusion should also include time for group members to clear away materials/equipment, or clean up any mess that has been made.

Learning to take responsibility for tools, equipment and materials is an important part of any form of group work, and generally this part of the session should precede the formal conclusion. Tidying and clearing away not only teaches desirable work/activity skills, but also reinforces concepts of co-operation, responsibility and shared commitment.

Evaluation

After a session has been concluded the staff involved need to review actual performance and achievements against the original session plan. This evaluation takes two forms: evaluation of each group members' performance, and evaluation of the performance of the staff in meeting the teaching objectives. Evaluation of group members' performance need not be particularly detailed, but does need to be sensitive enough to monitor changes and progress. An example of one method of recording this information is shown in Figure 9.6 on page 178.

Evaluation of staff performance and the achievement of objectives is best carried out verbally, but it is possible to use a written checklist. Any method of evaluation should include questions such as:

Did the session run as planned?
If not, was this a conscious reaction to group members' needs, or an accidental occurrence?
Was the session successful in achieving its objectives?
What problems were encountered, and how were they dealt with?
Could these problems have been managed more effectively?
Did the session conclude with everyone feeling satisfied with the group experience?
Which parts of the session were best and worst?
What mistakes were made?
What would have made the session better?
What changes need to be made before the session runs again?

Ultimately, evaluation is as useful as staff allow it to be. If it is carried out without any reference back to the running of the session, then it is ineffective; if it leads to better training opportunities for clients, and helps staff to refine and develop their teaching skills, then it is very useful.

MANIPULATION OF THE TEACHING ENVIRONMENT

Certain aspects of the environment can be manipulated to create a variety of moods and atmospheres within groups. The most powerful environmental manipulators are:

(1) the arrangement of rooms and seating patterns,
(2) space and size,
(3) colour and light levels,
(4) sound.

Arrangement of rooms

The arrangement of tables, chairs and equipment within a room can significantly influence the way in which that room is used, and underline the conceptual differences between work, social and recreational activities. The type of furniture available is the first influence on a room. Upright chairs and high tables suggest work-related activities, while low, easy chairs and side tables suggest a more informal, socially orientated group. The way in which the furniture/seating patterns are arranged is the next area of influence. Work groups may need several high tables at which different activities can be carried out. In these instances clients are usually seated, while staff stand (or sit and move around the group regularly) reinforcing a supervisory relationship through the differences in posture. Socially orientated groups are more likely to have low chairs in a circle or semicircle, and to have staff seated as group members, promoting greater feelings of equality and informality. Recreational activities may dispense with seating arrangements altogether, and by having only a few chairs available at various points of the room may encourage everyone to move, participate and mix with their colleagues. If various types of sports and play equipment are being used in recreational groups, then the arrangement of this equipment should enhance, not inhibit, progress from one activity to another.

Room space and size

The size of a room and the space available can be factors which can work either for or against the success of a group. Some groups cannot run without adequate space, while others benefit from the feelings of personal security and group identity that can be created by small, appropriately furnished rooms. Activities concerned with encouraging responses and interactions can be difficult to run in an inappropriately sized room, e.g. a large, echoing games hall, but equally undesirable behaviours can result from teaching environments which are too cramped. Ideally, all teaching environments should be large enough to accommodate everyone in the group for the chosen activity, but no larger. If different-sized rooms are not available, then screens or floor-to-ceiling curtains can be used to increase flexibility.

Colour and light

Colour and light levels are often neglected as tools for shaping the environment and effecting performance. Bright, cheerful colours can transform a dull or cold room, and with it raise the attitudes and motivation of people working there; bright colours used in rooms associated with less preferred activities, such as work training, can create a more positive attitude in group members. Pink or peachy shades in self-care areas are most flattering to skin shades, and can therefore enhance appearance, and neutral or pastel shades in all areas can promote a more relaxed and informal environment. An additional benefit of using different colours in different areas is that it makes it easier to identify rooms/areas and (if storage is colour-coded) makes it easier for individuals to participate in tidying away and storing equipment.

Carefully chosen blinds and curtains can be used to lower or diffuse light levels, aiding relaxation and informality. Drawing curtains or pulling down blinds on dark, wintry days can also make the room seem more inviting and secure. Overhead fluorescent lighting is good for general work groups, but softer lighting, achieved through lamps or dimmer switches, allows much more flexibility of room mood. With appropriate light fittings, coloured, low-wattage light bulbs can, for example, successfully transform a large hall into a club room. Changes to lighting systems can, of course, be expensive, but in planning new developments flexible lighting systems should always be considered part of the therapeutic environment.

GROUP LEADERSHIP AND MANAGEMENT

All staff working in groups need to be aware of the different roles they are expected to adopt. Leaders must be able to command the attention of the group, and be able to move the group through the activity to the achievement of the sessional goals, but they cannot do this alone. Whatever role the leader adopts, the helpers within the group need to mirror and support it. The main roles that can be adopted are:

Social model

This involves demonstrating the social behaviours that group members need to acquire. Many social behaviours, e.g. using 'please' and 'thank you', are generally applicable to all situations, but social behaviour specific to certain situations may need to be clearly defined. Staff acting as social models are only credible if they demonstrate the same standards of behaviour that they expect their clients to acquire, so social modelling needs to be a role that is consciously adopted whenever social or training contact occurs.

Physical model

Like social modelling, staff within groups also need to physically demonstrate actions and procedures that need to be carried out. It is, for example, inappropriate for staff to refuse to join in an activity if they are meant to be modelling desirable behaviours to their clients.

Physical modelling occurs on two levels. Firstly, particular actions, tasks or techniques may need to be demonstrated clearly as part of the teaching process. This includes always demonstrating the *safe* method work, rather than using short cuts which, if copied by a client, could be dangerous. Secondly, staff are physical models of appropriate appearance, which ranges from demonstrating good self-care and appearance skills, to reinforcing the use of protective clothing in certain activities.

Explainer

Staff within a group are responsible for ensuring that group members understand what is required. This means being able to express ideas or instructions clearly and effectively (without being patronising), varying the tone, volume and cadence of the voice to emphasise the importance of various comments, and to make effective use non-verbal communication, e.g. posture, gesture, signs and facial expressions.

Encourager

Group members need to be encouraged to participate and achieve as much as possible, and staff need to be able to know how much encouragement each person needs (and when to give it).

Controller

Any group needs to feel that those leading it are in control, and can deal with any disruptions that may occur. In addition to this, staff need to be able to manipulate the direction of the group to keep it close to planned teaching objectives, and to keep clients working towards individual goals.

Innovator

Closed groups can be very static, so staff also need to be innovators. This need not necessarily involve developing new projects and activities, but does require them to bring new experiences and ideas into the group.

Trainer

Obviously anyone involved in group work needs to know why the group is running, what is to be achieved and how individuals are to work towards planned goals. In addition, staff should also be skilled in a range of teaching techniques, and understand how to meet individual learning difficulties.

Observer

If group work aims are to be met, staff within the group must be able to observe and evaluate what happens, and keep appropriate records.

However, the most important requirement in effective group leadership is good communication between all staff. Close working relationships make everything much easier to achieve, and make the group experience more enjoyable for both clients and staff.

TIMETABLE PLANNING

Therapeutic group work is usually organised into timetables, with individual work being fitted around regular commitments. Timetables should reflect different levels of need, and make full use of all the staff available. To provide a comprehensive training timetable, four levels are necessary:

(1) basic training activities,
(2) intermediate training activities,
(3) advanced training activities,
(4) maintenance activities.

Levels (1)–(3) provide groups related to the training needs described in Chapters 6, 7 and 8. A maintenance activities timetable is needed for clients who need to consolidate their current skills rather than follow an active programme of development, and it should therefore include a variety of experiences, the opportunity to practise existing skills and the facility to decide what to do and when to do it.

Using an interrelated set of timetables means that individuals are initially referred to the timetable that best meets their overall needs, but they can also be referred to other timetable levels, for specific sessions. For example, a client placed on the intermediate timetable might attend one group from the advanced timetable, seven from the intermediate timetable and two from the maintenance timetable. The advantage of an interlinked timetable is the flexibility to meet the specific needs of each individual in groups that are appropriate to their developmental level. The process of developing four inter-related and graded training timetables is uncomplicated, but requires a lot of time for planning objectives and co-ordinating programmes. The main steps are described below.

Dividing clients into broad ability/needs groups

After defining the differences between the four timetable levels, clients should be placed within the timetable level most suited to the majority of their needs. In doing this there should be some indication of each client's likely need for access to groups from other timetable levels, e.g.:

Basic	Intermediate	Advanced	Maintenance
John (+I)	Jane (+A & M)	Anne	Ivy (+A)
Jenny (+M)	Violet (+B & M)	Andy (+I)	Henry
Trevor	Linda (+A)	Bert (+M)	Iris (+I)

This will give some idea of the proportional demand for each level of training.

Establishing group work needs for each timetable level

The next step in planning is to define the broad areas of function and skill that are relevant to everyone in the whole client group, and can be included in all timetable levels, e.g. physical function, appearance or cognition, and then to identify the developmental levels required for each of the four timetables, as shown in the brief example in Table 9.1.

Table 9.1

Area	Basic	Intermediate	Advanced	Maintenance
Physical function	Basic movement	Exercise/ Keep-fit	Sport/ fitness	Mobility
	Positioning	Stamina	Health care	Preventative care
Meal preparation	Sensory baking	Snacks and drinks	Meals and shopping	Baking
Vocational skills	Toy play	Construc- tional work	Work training	Fund-raising
Appearance	Body image	Personal care	Personal appearance	General grooming
Cognition	Perception	Concept formation	Literacy and numeracy	Reality orientation

The areas included in each breakdown/profile can come from assessments, collation of information from various staff, or from developmental profiles. There is no right or wrong profile — profiles have to be relevant to each client group and their local community.

Once a complete profile of group training needs has been established, the types of training groups needed, and the creative media to be used, should be obvious. Some groups, such as physical function groups, are clearly defined separate entities; others may be composites of several smaller areas, e.g. concept groups can include self-image, colour, descriptive vocabulary and perceptual development. Certain creative media may be more effective in achieving training goals than any other means, and decisions about which creative media to use (and why) should be taken at this stage. Additionally, priorities must be decided for each group, in terms of the number of clients likely to benefit from the training, and the numbers of staff available.

Establishing the type of individual teaching required for each timetable level

Individual training needs can be identified through the same profiling exercise used to determine group work needs, although only general lists of training needs can be made; each client will have additional, more specific needs that cannot be identified through the group process.

Deciding on the structure of the daily timetable

Times for groups and individual sessions have to be fitted into a daily work structure. There are many, many different permutations, such as the example shown below; this timetable assumes that there is some flexibility in working hours, i.e. some staff work 8.00–4.00, while others work 9.00–5.00. Any daily timetable has to take into account the needs of the group, recognised priorities for training, and the availability of staff.

Example timetable

8.00–9.00	Individual self-care programmes.
9.00–9.30	Handover meeting, discussing changes in training and decisions from planning meetings.
9.30–9.45	Preparation for Group 1 or individual work.
9.45–10.15	Tea break with clients.
10.15–11.45	Group 1 or individual work.
11.45–12.45	Lunch with clients (individual work), or record-keeping for Group 1.
12.45–1.30	Staff lunch.
1.30–2.00	Preparation for Groups 2 & 3 or individual work
2.00–3.00	Group 2 or individual work.
3.00–3.30	Tea break with clients.
3.30–4.30	Group 3 or individual work.
4.30–5.00	Evaluation and record-keeping for Groups 2 and 3.

Deciding on the final make-up of the timetables

Once the daily format has been decided, groups and individual sessions can be fitted into the four timetable levels. However, before this can be done the maximum number of clients per group, the number of staff required per group and the number of staff available, must all be identified.

The maximum number of clients per group depends on the type of group and the ability of the clients. Generally, groups which are teaching new skills should aim to have a 1 : 2 (Basic), 1 : 3 (Intermediate), or 1 : 4 (Advanced) staff : client ratio, and have no more than four to six clients in the group. Groups that provide opportunites to practise existing skills, or are teaching social and interaction skills, should aim for the same staff : client ratios, but the groups can be larger (i.e. ten to twelve people). Staffing ratios and group size on the maintenance timetable will vary according to the abilities and needs of the individuals. Limiting the size of training groups can be hard when there are many people who would benefit from attendance, but the quality of training is directly related to the number of people involved, and to provide an effective training service the quality of training must be maintained.

The number of staff available places an obvious constraint on the amount of training that can be offered. To make a success of any training system, two things are essential: (a) that there are sufficient staff to ensure that training groups and individual sessions can be maintained at all times, and (b) that staff have sufficient administrative and development time to support the practical training they provide. Firstly, to ensure that there is sufficient cover for the training sessions, one member of staff should be left free during each main group or individual session on the timetable. This 'free' member of staff should participate in all groups and individual programmes that run during their 'free' time, so that if any other member of staff is absent they can take over their responsibilities. At times when all timetabled staff are present the 'free' person either provides extra help in one of the timetabled sessions, or works individually with a client who has no planned timetable activity. It can be difficult to justify the inclusion of 'free' staff in timetable planning when staff resources are limited, but trial periods can be used to show the improvement that occurs when appropriate staffing structures are adopted.

Secondly, staff involved in intensive training need administrative time (to attend meetings, write reports, keep records, carry out assessments, select and order treatment resources and maintain routine departmental records) and self-development time (reading, tutorials, lectures, attendance at courses). Restricting administrative time reduces the quality of training provided, and can affect the accuracy of the information used to make decisions about training

169

goals. Providing little, if any, self-development time, inhibits the development of skill and can have a detrimental effect on morale. Self-development and administrative time are so important that some professional staffing reports recommend that only approximately 50 per cent of each person's working time should be spent in direct client contact.

Safety aspects also need to be considered at this stage. These could range from having the right equipment/environment for the training session to having the correct staff : client ratio. There must certainly be enough staff to cater for clients' needs without exposing other people to danger; e.g. there should be enough staff to take someone to the toilet without leaving the remaining clients unsupervised, if to do so would be dangerous. The more distant activities are from other staff, the more thought needs to be given to appropriate staffing levels.

Examples of each timetable level, showing group sizes, the minimum amount of individual work possible, and staff allocations, are shown in Figures 9.2–9.5. The advanced timetable shows only the general division of the working day; in such a timetable, clients would work through priority areas for training, and the actual content of each individual or group work session would regularly change. These timetables, excluding the advanced level, have been used by a department of ten staff to provide a training system for approximately 45 people.

Setting objectives for each group

It is impossible to provide a comprehensive training system without using aims and objectives. Clearly defined aims and objectives for each training activity provide staff with a clear framework to work within, and specific goals to work towards. Different people understand different things by 'aims' and 'objectives', and although it is relatively easy to define aims and objectives for individual training programmes, it is less easy to do so for group work. We have found the following definitions the most helpful:

(1) *Aims* explain why a particular creative medium/activity has been selected instead of any other, and the relevance it has to the development of overall function.

(2) *Long-term/terminal/training objectives* describe the level of skill or function (in various areas) that all group members will

Figure 9.2: Basic Timetable

	MONDAY	TUESDAY	WEDNESDAY	THURSDAY	FRIDAY
8.30–9.00	FEEDING	ASSESSMENTS	AND	TRAINING	PROGRAMMES
9.00–9.30	HANDOVER	OF	INFORMATION	RELATED TO	TRAINING
9.30–9.45	PREPARATION	FOR	MORNING	TRAINING	SESSIONS
9.45–10.15	TEA	WITH	CLIENTS	IN	TEA BAR
10.15–11.45	KEEP FIT 7 clients 3 staff INDIVIDUAL WORK	ACTION SINGING 8 clients 3 staff INDIVIDUAL WORK	PETO GROUP 4 clients 4 staff INDIVIDUAL WORK	LUNCH COOKING 4 clients 2 staff INDIVIDUAL WORK	SENSORY PLAY 6 clients 2 staff INDIVIDUAL WORK
11.45–12.45	LUNCH	LUNCH	LUNCH	LUNCH	LUNCH
12.45–2.00	RECORDS,	NOTES,	REPORTS,	AND	ASSESSMENTS
2.00–3.00	CREATIVE GROUP 8 clients 3 staff INDIVIDUAL WORK	BAKING 4 clients 2 staff INDIVIDUAL WORK	MOVEMENT 7 clients 3 staff INDIVIDUAL WORK	TOY PLAY 7 clients 2 staff INDIVIDUAL WORK	SWIMMING 1:1 ratio INDIVIDUAL WORK
3.00–3.30	TEA	WITH	CLIENTS	IN	TEA BAR
3.30–4.30	STAFF TRAINING	BAKING (continued) INDIVIDUAL WORK	INDIVIDUAL WORK	INDIVIDUAL WORK	SWIMMING (continued) or ADMIN TIME
4.30–5.00		GROUP	WORK	RECORDS	& NOTES

Figure 9.3: Intermediate Timetable

	MONDAY	TUESDAY	WEDNESDAY	THURSDAY	FRIDAY
8.30–9.00	SELF	CARE	TRAINING	PROGRAMMES	& ASSESSMENTS
9.00–9.30	HANDOVER	OF	INFORMATION	RELATED TO	TRAINING
9.30–9.45	PREPARATION	FOR	MORNING	TRAINING	SESSIONS
9.45–10.15	TEA	WITH	CLIENTS	IN	TEA BAR
10.15–11.45	WORK TRAINING 12 clients 3 staff / LUNCH COOKING 3 clients 1 staff / INDIVIDUAL WORK	SINGING 11 clients 3 staff / LUNCH COOKING 3 clients 1 staff / INDIVIDUAL WORK	BAKING 4 clients 1 staff / GARDENING 4 clients 1 staff / SINGING (see Figure 9.5)	WORK TRAINING 12 clients 3 staff / CONCEPTS 6 clients 2 staff / INDIVIDUAL WORK	SENSORY WORK 6 clients 2 staff / SPORTS GROUP 8 clients 2 staff / INDIVIDUAL WORK
11.45–12.45	LUNCH	LUNCH	LUNCH	LUNCH	LUNCH
12.45–2.00	RECORDS,	NOTES,	REPORTS,	AND	ASSESSMENTS
2.00–3.00	KEEP FIT 10 clients 3 staff / CONCEPTS 6 clients 2 staff / INDIVIDUAL WORK	LISTENING 6 clients 1 staff / GARDENING 4 clients 1 staff / APPEARANCE 4 clients 1 staff	BAKING 8 clients 2 staff / SELF CARE 8 clients 3 staff / INDIVIDUAL WORK	CREATIVE WORK 7 clients 2 staff / APPEARANCE 4 clients 1 staff / HORSE-RIDING 1:1 ratio	SOCIAL SKILLS 1. 10 clients 2 staff / SOCIAL SKILLS 2. 7 clients 2 staff / GARDENING 4 clients 1 staff
3.00–3.30	TEA	WITH	CLIENTS	IN	TEA BAR
3.30–4.30	STAFF TRAINING	APPEARANCE 4 clients 1 staff / CONCEPTS 4 clients 1 staff / GARDENING 5 clients 1 staff	CONCEPTS 4 clients 1 staff / HOBBIES 8 clients 4 staff / INDIVIDUAL WORK	REALITY ORIENTATION 5 clients 2 staff / APPEARANCE 4 clients 1 staff	ADMIN TIME
4.30–5.00	GROUP	GROUP	WORK	RECORDS	& NOTES

Figure 9.4: Advanced Timetable

	MONDAY	TUESDAY	WEDNESDAY	THURSDAY	FRIDAY
8.30–9.00	SUPERVISION	OF SELF CARE	AND	DOMESTIC	ROUTINES
9.00–9.30	HANDOVER	OF	INFORMATION	RELATED TO	TRAINING
9.30–9.45	PREPARATION	FOR	MORNING	TRAINING	SESSIONS
9.45–10.15	TEA	BREAK	AND	DISCUSSION	GROUP
10.15–11.45	PROJECT WORK (Project work is undertaken individually, or in small groups of up to 6 clients: 2 staff, depending on the needs of each client.			PROJECT WORK	PROJECT WORK
11.45–12.45 12.45–2.00	} LUNCH	PLANNING, ...	PREPARATION, ...	AND	EATING
2.00–3.30	PRACTICAL SESSION (Practical work is related to project areas covered in morning sessions, and like the project work groups, the work is undertaken individually or in small groups, depending on the needs of the client.)	PRACTICAL SESSION	PRACTICAL SESSION	PRACTICAL SESSION	PRACTICAL SESSION
3.30–4.30	STAFF TRAINING	→	→	→	
4.30–5.00	NOTES, ...	REPORTS, ...	AND	ASSESSMENTS

Figure 9.5: Maintenance Timetable

	MONDAY	TUESDAY	WEDNESDAY	THURSDAY	FRIDAY
8.30–9.00	SELF	CARE	PROGRAMMES	AND	ASSESSMENTS
9.00–9.30	HANDOVER	OF	INFORMATION	RELATED TO	TRAINING
9.30–9.45	PREPARATION	FOR	MORNING	TRAINING	SESSIONS
9.45–10.15	TEA	WITH	CLIENTS	IN	TEA BAR
10.15–11.45	HAIR CARE 7 clients 1 staff	DRAMA/SOCIAL SKILLS 20 clients 4 staff	SINGING 22 clients 3 staff	HAIRDRESSING Appointments	FUNDRAISING 15 clients 2 staff
11.45–12.45	LUNCH	LUNCH	LUNCH	LUNCH	LUNCH
12.45–2.00	RECORDS,	REPORTS,	NOTES,	AND	ASSESSMENTS
2.00–3.00	GARDENING 10 clients 2 staff	MOBILITY 10 clients 2 staff	SELF CARE 14 clients 3 staff	MUSIC 15 clients 2 staff	DOMESTIC WORK 8 clients 1 staff
3.00–3.30	TEA	WITH	CLIENTS	IN	TEA BAR
3.30–4.30	STAFF TRAINING	REALITY ORIENTATION 4 clients 1 staff APPEARANCE 4 clients 1 staff	HOBBIES 10 clients 2 staff	LIBRARY 15 clients 2 staff	ADMIN TIME
4.30–5.00		GROUP	WORK	RECORDS	& NOTES

hopefully eventually achieve through regular participation and attendance.

(3) *Short-term/teaching/sessional objectives* describe the level of participation and the key teaching points for each group that runs. These objectives are very similar to the teaching objectives found in individual programmes, and should provide the framework for running any group. They will change from session to session, and need not include every long-term/terminal/training objective in every session plan.

An example of how a training group may be defined by its aims and both types of objectives is given below:

Example plan — play

Aim — To achieve sufficient mastery of cognitive, perceptual, social and motor skills, by taking individuals through progressively more complex stages of development, for participation in all aspects of daily life.

Long-term/terminal/training objectives

(1) The achievement of the highest possible degree of independent motor control and co-ordination, e.g. head control, crawling and balancing.
(2) The achievement of skilful hand function and fine motor control.
(3) Consolidation and extension of all visual skills such as tracking, scanning, object selection and focusing.
(4) Competence in exploring the environment through the senses, especially tactile experience, e.g. sand, water, textures.
(5) Maximum competence in social play, e.g. solitary play, parallel play, co-operative play, associative play and imaginative play.
(6) Competence in the understanding and use of environmental concepts, e.g. shape and form constancy, qualities and properties of different materials, colour and figure–ground perception.
(7) Understanding of the consequences of actions, e.g. splashing water or bouncing a ball.

Short-term/teaching/sessional objectives

Each person will:
(1) name or identify other people working in the group;
(2) distinguish between soft and hard objects;
(3) distinguish between wet and dry materials;
(4) discriminate between yellow, blue and red objects;

175

(5) manipulate and successfully position one large, one medium and one small object;

(6) maintain eye contact, and visually track a large, medium and small object.

Objectives should take into account physical function, sensory function, communication skills, socialisation skills, cognitive function, expression of emotion and vocational skills.

Deciding who will attend each group

Once the timetable has been organised, individuals can be referred to each group. Those groups where there are too many people should keep waiting lists, so that when a place becomes vacant, or additional staff become available, these clients can be included. Referral to various groups should form part of the discussion at client planning meetings. During this process each client will gradually have a timetable built up that is unique, and based on his individual needs. At this stage each individual will have regular times during the week when he has no timetabled groups, and these periods can then be used for individual training by various staff.

Planning individual work in relation to the group work commitments

Once the group work timetables have been completed, names can be pencilled in against the individual work sessions given on the timetables. There will obviously be some degree of priority attached to deciding who is referred for individual training sessions, but given that two or three individual programmes can be carried out by one member of staff in each group work period, there should be sufficient time available to provide a number of people with individual training. Additionally, other staff outside the training situation may get involved in the provision of individual teaching, and further increase the opportunities available.

Deciding on the resources needed for each group/individual session

All training activities require equipment and/or material resources to

176

be successful, particularly if creative media are used. For some training sessions the correct facilities are essential, so timetable planning also needs to ensure that required resources are available at the correct time. If space or resources are limited, the use of certain rooms/pieces of equipment may need to be carefully timetabled.

Deciding how to evaluate the timetable

There is no point in setting up a comprehensive training system if the work done is not evaluated. However, evaluation and record-keeping for a large group of people can be time-consuming, so it is useful to develop some means of recording the information that is required in the most economical way possible. One solution is to use a simple chart, recording general aspects of progress during training. The example shown in Figure 9.6 records:

(1) participation, i.e. whether each client carries out actions appropriate to the activity;
(2) behaviour, i.e. whether each client showed appropriate social behaviour and interaction;
(3) attitude, i.e. each client's reaction to the training activity;
(4) interaction, i.e. how well each client communicated and interacted with staff and group members;
(5) engagement, i.e. what proportion of time was each client actively engaged in the training activity.

If brief headings such as these are used in a record chart they must be defined in order to avoid confusion and inaccuracy. The definitions for 'participation' are shown below:

(1) *Minimal*, i.e. does not perform actions compatible with the activity despite staff prompting or praise, *or* occasionally performs actions compatible with the activity either spontaneously or with staff prompting.
(2) *Passive*, i.e. performs actions compatible with the activity but in response to staff prompting or praise *and* maintains these actions throughout the session.
(3) *Participates when appropriate*, i.e. performs actions compatible with the activity throughout the session, *and* does not need excessive prompting or praise but may need instructions.
(4) *Participates spontaneously*, i.e. performs actions compatible

177

Figure 9.6

DAY		SESSION	Partici-pation					Behaviour					Interaction					Attitude to group					Engage-ment					NAME: CHART BEGINS: COMMENTS:* To include relevant information e.g. had fit, change of group leader (where this affects performance), etc.	INITIALS
			Minimal	Passive	Participates when appropriate	Participates spontaneously	Over-participates	Disruptive of the group	Disruptive of own work	Appropriate	Deals well with minor problems	Deals well with major problems	Minimal	With staff only	With staff and group members	Initiates interaction with staff	Initiates interaction with anyone	Refuses to join in group	Joins in when encouraged	Co-operates willingly	Enthusiastic about group	Dominates group by enthusiasm	Minimal	Works spasmodically	Works consistently	Perserverative and inflexible	Works at familiar tasks only		
MON	am																												
	pm																												
TUES	am																												
	pm																												
WEDS	am																												
	pm																												
THURS	am																												
	pm																												
FRI	am																												
	pm																												
MON	am																												
	pm																												
TUES	am																												
	pm																												
WEDS	am																												
	pm																												
THURS	am																												
	pm																												
FRI	am																												
	pm																												

with the activity throughout the session, with minimal prompting, following initial instructions.

(5) *Over-participation*, i.e. performs actions compatible with the activity throughout the session *but* carries these actions out to excess and fails to respond to staff prompting and instructions in an appropriate manner.

Charts can save time in recording routine information, but they need to be supplemented by additional information and reports. Keeping records, recording progress and regularly referring back to the agreed training objectives, provides an effective way of evaluating any training system.

SUMMARY

Group work is often an under-valued form of training because of its association with creative media and the size of training groups; people with little involvement in group work tend to see the diversional or occupational aspects of the activity, but not the therapeutic nature of the work. This type of training opportunity is very effective in meeting a range of needs, but only if realistic staff : client ratios and group sizes can be achieved. Overloading therapeutic groups and reducing the staff : client ratios effectively reduces any benefit that may be derived from them, and has a marked effect on staff morale. Ideally, any training situation needs sufficient staff to run a well-structured group work timetable, as well as to provide individual training opportunities.

Further information

P. Douglas, *Group Work Practice* (Tavistock, London and New York, 1981).

M.B. Miles, *Learning to Work in Groups* (Teachers College Press, New York, 1971).

10

Group Work Activity Ideas

Learning is more enjoyable if creative media are used.

The rationale for the use of creative media in a training timetable is that clients are more receptive, and better motivated to learn, if teaching is presented in an enjoyable and interesting manner. Therapeutic activities are usually selected either by:

(1) choosing an activity that is known to be enjoyable to group members, and structuring that activity to meet training needs; *OR*
(2) choosing an activity which will meet therapeutic needs, and then structuring it in a positive way.

Activities can be used both generally and specifically. Generally, any activity should provide informal opportunities to generalise conceptual and practical skills. This is usually done through inter-action so it is important that any contact is open-ended and uses questions rather than statements of fact. For example, in a cooking session, or at mealtimes, this informal teaching should take the form of:

'What do we need to eat with?', 'Where are the knives and forks kept?', and 'Are there enough knives and forks for four people?' instead of 'Please get four knives and forks from the drawer.'

180

'What do we need to put the food on?', 'What colour are the plates/bowls/cups?', and 'How many plates/bowls/cups do we need?' instead of 'Please get the plates/bowls/cups from the cupboard.'

'What colour is the tablecloth?', 'Is the tablecloth plain or patterned?', and 'Can you tell what we're going to eat from the smell?' instead of 'Dinner's ready!'

For more specific use, each activity should be analysed to identify its training potential; very few, if any, activities can meet all training requirements, so it is important to be able to evaluate the relative merits of a variety of media. Analysis should consider:

(1) *Physical function* — i.e. does the activity maintain and/or develop physical function, range of movement, gross motor skills, fine motor skills, balance, mobility and stamina, and how can this be developed further?

(2) *Sensory function* — i.e. does the activity stimulate sensory development, enhance perception and increase understanding, and how can this be developed further?

(3) *Cognitive function* — i.e. does the activity help the client to understand and follow instructions, make decisions, form concepts, learn, plan and apply, and how can this be developed further?

(4) *Communication* — i.e. does the activity encourage verbal and non-verbal communication, speech, hearing/listening, conversation, reading and writing, and how can this be developed further?

(5) *Socialisation* — i.e. does the activity help to increase social skills, tolerance and positive interactions, and how can this be developed further?

(6) *Self-reliance* — i.e. does the activity enhance independent living, maturity and social development, and how can this be developed further?

(7) *Work skills* — i.e. does the activity provide opportunities to develop co-operation, perseverance, speed, reliability, consistency and responsibility, and how can this be developed further?

Once a therapeutic activity has been chosen, particularly if it forms a regular part of a training timetable, it needs to be used flexibly in order to maintain the interest and motivation that it was originally chosen to stimulate! Staff responsible for running therapeutic groups should therefore explore every possible use of the basic medium, so that clients can experience everything that the activity offers. These new ideas and new applications for familiar activities can be gleaned from the many books on creative media that are available, but flexibility of approach also applies to the way materials and resources are used within the groups. For example, even a simple yoghurt pot can be used in may activities; as a container, in gardening or cooking; for building or stacking; for sorting, matching and counting; as skittles; for music making (by filling with sand or pasta, and sealing); for sand and water play; for imaginative play (e.g. as noses); for printing and collage work; for constructional work and model-making or for measuring volume.

Each activity chosen should be incorporated into a sessional plan, which highlights certain aspects of the overall aim and objectives for the group; this does not need to be formally written down, although there are advantages in doing so. Any method of planning (mentally, scribbled notes, discussions with other staff, etc.) is acceptable as long as it leads to well-run groups which meet both individual and training needs. However, making written plans is certainly advisable for staff who are inexperienced in running groups, or who have responsibility for training other staff. Sessional plans should resemble individual teaching programmes in format, but need only contain brief reminders of planned work. The remainder of this chapter looks at the potential of various activities, including examples of possible sessional plans. In reality all these sessional plans would need to relate back to agreed aims and long-term/terminal/training objectives (see Chapter 9).

MOVEMENT

Physical movement sessions are most frequently used within basic training timetables for clients who have restricted or underdeveloped movement patterns, but some degree of motor control. This type of physical input is often called developmental movement, because the exercises aim to develop relationships and communication patterns as well as to stimulate physical function. Much of the work requires close physical contact (staff may have to use their bodies as 'bridges' or 'tunnels'), and can therefore also be useful in developing body awareness, and the use of touch in relationships. Participation in this activity may be enhanced by motor control, co-operation, the ability to copy and the ability to respond to verbal instructions.

A lot of emphasis is placed on improving the suppleness and use of the trunk, so sessions include a high proportion of floor work; for this reason developmental movement sessions need to take place in an area with clean, comfortable and safe flooring. A session progresses through the stages of normal development, i.e. supine, prone, sitting, standing and walking, providing increased help and support wherever and whenever needed. More advanced use of movement, where clients can initiate their own actions, can be included as appropriate. The nature of developmental movement is such that it requires a high staff ratio, so that each client can be safely and securely helped through each exercise. Ideally this should mean at least a 1 : 1 staff : client ratio.

Other forms of physical exercise and movement should also be included, particularly play activities. Physical play activities provide opportunities to experiment with different methods of movement, and different spatial experiences. Soft play equipment provides a safe yet stimulating environment (made up of inflatables for bouncing on, water mattresses, ball pools, swing chairs, etc.), that also aids sensory development. This equipment can be expensive to buy, or even hire, but is a worthwhile investment.

EXAMPLE GROUP PLAN NO. 1

Activity

Developmental movement.

Group details

Six people + six staff for approximately 1 hour.

Teaching objectives

(1) Each person will work through all exercises as independently as possible.
(2) Each person will experience a variety of functional positions.
(3) Each person will experience different types of physical contact and touch.
(4) Each person will experiment with body and spatial awareness through different exercises.

Equipment needed

Mats, rugs, cassette recorder, quiet music and songs.

Presentation

(1) Sit in a circle, with each member of staff supporting a client (as shown) and introduce everyone by name.

(2) Sing along to songs, while gently rocking each client.
(3) Explain what is going to happen in the group, then lie each client down and massage muscles as a warm-up to the activity. Encourage each client to massage his partner.

Content

(1) Lie with feet pointing to the centre of the circle, and roll around the room (a) individually, (b) in pairs, with staff partner either alongside client, or lying head to head and holding hands, and (c) with each partner rolling the other person (if possible).
(2) Sit up with partner sitting behind the client with legs astride, supporting the client's upper body (as in 'Presentation' no. 1). Rock gently from side to side.
(3) Sit opposite partner, with legs astride, feet touching and hands held, then rock gently backwards and forwards.
(4) Working with another pair, lay one client on a rug in supine position, and pull the rug around the room. Repeat for the other client.
(5) Working in the same group of four, put a client on the rug in supine position. Staff hold either end of the rug so that the person is safely cradled, e.g.:

and (a) gently pull/lift the rug over foam wedges and (b) gently swing the rug from side to side.

(6) Staying in the same group of four people, one member of staff takes up a position on hands and knees resembling a tunnel, e.g.:

The other member of staff prompts both clients to crawl through the 'tunnel'.

(7) Adapt the 'tunnel' to become a 'bridge', e.g.:

and prompt clients to crawl over the 'bridge'.

(8) With two staff to each client, and using appropriate equipment, allow each person to stand for as long as he can tolerate.

Conclusions

(1) Return to original pairs, and sit in position described in Presentation no. 1. Sing along to songs, while gently rocking each client.

(2) Lie each client down and massage muscles, relax each client.

(3) Relaxation to quiet music.

185

PHYSICAL EXERCISE

Fitness, suppleness and mobility, however limited, are important for any person, irrespective of lifestyle and environment. There are marked physiological benefits to be gained from exercise, in addition to the functional, psychological and social advantages. Apart from basic movement sessions, physical exercise groups usually involve fairly mobile clients who are likely to be following an intermediate training timetable. Clients following advanced living skills timetables also need physical exercise sessions, but their sessions will probably include more emphasis on using community sports facilities, and on understanding why and how to keep fit. Participation in this activity may be enhanced by competence in all aspects of basic motor skill, understanding of instructions, the ability to copy and work through exercises with little physical help, and the ability to work with other group members.

Most intermediate exercise groups are reasonably large, e.g. ten to twelve people, and there should be at least one member of staff working in these groups with sufficient knowledge of anatomy, physiology and various conditions to ensure safe training for every group member. For example, staff should be aware of the possibility of atlanto-axial instability in people with Down's syndrome, and the special precautions that may be necessary.

Educational rhythmics (S.G. Moule, 1984) is a particular approach to physical exercise, which aims to stimulate and develop a variety of skills related to movement by synchronising purposeful body movements with verbal instructions, verses, songs and music. Body actions mime or represent the meaning of the words used, and can be useful in consolidating the use of gesture and body language as a means of communication. Yoga and other techniques or approaches can also be useful to include in physical exercise sessions.

Whichever approach is used for sessions of this type, variety is just as important as in more 'creative' media. Some exercises need to be repeated regularly, but too much repetition leads to boredom. Use a variety of teaching media such as videos, exercise tapes, dancing and games, as well as experimenting with environmental changes, e.g. using torches in darkened rooms, visiting sports facilities, moving outdoors when the weather allows.

EXAMPLE GROUP PLAN NO. 2

Activity

Keep-fit.

Group details

Twelve people + three staff for approximately 1½ hours.

Teaching objectives

(1) Each person will participate in a wide variety of exercises.
(2) Each person will use different pieces of equipment successfully.
(3) Each person will work individually, in pairs and in a group.
(4) Each person will follow verbal instructions correctly.

Equipment needed

Balls, hoops, games sticks (e.g. hockey sticks), ribbon sticks, torch, bean bags, video and exercise tapes, cassette recorder and selection of music.

Presentation

(1) Introduce activity, and prompt gentle warm-up exercises.
(2) Introduce games that bring clients into close contact with others, e.g. passing a small ball held under the chin from person to person, or passing a matchbox from nose to nose.

Content

(1) Head and neck exercises, e.g. following the light a torch makes on walls and ceiling in a darkened room.
(2) Trunk exercises, e.g. bending, twisting, stretching.
(3) Leg and foot exercises, e.g. stretching, pointing, kicking.
(4) Arm and hand exercises, e.g. stretching, waving, punching.
(5) Dancing to videotape, copying dance exercises that incorporate the movements practised in (1)–(4).
(6) Divide into pairs and work with hoops, passing hoops over partner's head and down to ground and vice-versa, to encourage stretching and balance.
(7) Exchange hoops for ribbon sticks, followed by (a) individual work to music, (b) mirror copying partner and (c) following the movement of partner's ribbon with various parts of the body, e.g. arms, eyes, head.
(8) Group ribbon waving exercises — copying leader in time to music.

187

(9) Balance exercises and games, e.g. carrying egg and spoon, or beanbag on head, around the room and over a series of objects.
(10) Team games.

Conclusions

(1) Divide into pairs, and massage each other.
(2) Lie down and carry out relaxation exercises.
(3) End by listening to a quiet piece of music.

COOKING

Very few individuals fail to respond to cooking as a therapeutic activity, because it is a medium which is actively reinforcing. It is also a very versatile medium, which can be carried out at varying levels of complexity, to meet a wide range of training needs. Depending on whether or not cooking is used as a sensory experience, a teaching medium, or as part of an advanced training programme, participation in this activity is enhanced by different skills. For example, in basic training cooking requires competence in basic motor skills, an ability to interact with the environment and competence in visual and perceptual discrimination, whereas cooking as part of an advanced training timetable requires numeracy, some degree of literacy, competence in conceptual/sequential learning and an understanding of basic procedures and nutritional values.

In basic training programmes, cooking provides opportunities to practise fine motor skills, develop co-ordination and participate in sensory experiences, through the use of high-contact processes such as rubbing-in, kneading or rolling pastry. Very few tools are used by the clients, and the responsibility for cooking and safety is usually taken by staff. The main emphasis is on concept formation, sensory development and a greater understanding of food preparation and sequencing.

In intermediate sessions there is a greater emphasis on learning the technical skills associated with the handling of food. Sessions may still have a sensory component, but are more likely to include snack/drink and shared meal preparation as the teaching media. This involves learning how to use preparation and cooking equipment safely, e.g. kettles, tin-openers, sharp knives and ovens, and also how to handle food. Each client works more independently, but under close staff supervision. Gadgets such as food processors and blenders may be used in order to assist independence, or to reduce the amount of time needed to produce the snack or meal.

Advanced training should enable each individual to plan, shop for and cook meals and snacks, and attend to the preparation of any type of food or drink. Because of this, as much time needs to be given to associated activities as to the cooking process itself. There may also be a greater reliance on convenience foods than in other training levels, and as clients become more independent, cooking sessions should be unsupervised.

At all levels, cooking processes can be considerably simplified by using balance rather than spring-loaded weighing scales, measuring spoons rather than ounces or grams, and cups instead of fluid ounces. However, all cooking groups within a timetable system should use the same types of measurement, in order to avoid confusion when a client moves from one timetable level to another. If at all possible the links between cookery sessions and the source of the materials, e.g. shops or garden, should be made clear, and if there is sufficient time the group should actually fetch the required ingredients themselves. Similarly, cooking sessions should include a wide range of experience, e.g. making yoghurt, bread, sweets and wine.

Cooking, as a creative activity, is a great socialiser, i.e. working closely with other people to produce something that not only tastes good, but also smells and looks good, usually precipitated some form of interaction. More specifically, cooking sessions can be structured to encourage socialisation by prompting clients to share their produce with others, in a process that becomes self-reinforcing, i.e. as each person offers his produce to others, he is thanked and receives reinforcement, and is thus more likely to repeat this process again. Socialisation in snack and meal cookery can involve inviting guests to share meals, and so can develop useful social skills.

EXAMPLE GROUP NO. 3

Activity

Sensory baking.

Group details

Six people and three staff for approximately 1½ hours.

Teaching objectives

(1) Each person will differentiate between broad sensory qualities,

189

e.g. wet/dry.
(2) Each person will name familiar objects and materials.
(3) Each person will demonstrate an understanding of sequencing,
e.g. putting on aprons and washing hands before preparation.
(4) Each person will participate in a range of sensory experiences.

Equipment needed

Cooking utensils and ingredients, aprons, ovens.

Presentation

(1) Introduce the activity either by explaining what is to be made,
or offering a choice or suitable recipes, e.g. anything that needs
hand mixing such as scones or pastry.
(2) Look at pictures of the finished items in cookery books.
(3) Carry out initial preparations, e.g. putting on aprons, washing
hands, lighting ovens.

Content

(1) Identify and get out any equipment required. Discuss how to use
any relevant equipment.
(2) Name the ingredients needed, and identify them by smell, taste,
touch and sight. Investigate the different properties of each
ingredient.
(3) Weigh out ingredients on balance scales. Each individual should
watch the scales and if possible identify when the correct weight
has been reached, i.e. when the ingredient pan moves downwards.
(4) Work through the recipe, mixing everything together.
Everything should be mixed in by hand — eggs, milk, currants;
and clients should be encouraged to describe what each ingredient feels like as it is mixed in.
(5) Investigate the feel of the baking tins before finished items are
put on or in them. Each client should then either watch or help
to put items in the oven; whatever their degree of participation
they should be aware of the heat of the oven.
(6) Washing up, with discussion of wet/dry and clean/dirty.

Conclusions

(1) Putting away clean equipment and ingredients, and cleaning
tables.
(2) Discussion of what has been made — ingredients, processes and
order of work.

(3) Identification of produce by its smell, and looking at the colour to see if food is cooked.

(4) Putting finished produce on plates and sharing with colleagues and friends.

PLAY AND DRAMA

Play and drama are interrelated media, used for training social, interaction and communication skills. Play sessions are usually used to guide or prompt a client through a desirable sequence of events or experiences, so that each client can learn more about his environment and their social group. Play sessions which are specifically sequenced to reflect daily living experiences, or real activities, are usually referred to as creative or imaginative play sessions. They are very useful for facilitating insight learning (colloquially referred to as 'aha' or 'penny-dropping' learning), and for teaching and/or underlining daily living sequences currently being taught through individual programmes. Drama, however, is usually used with clients who have learned regularly used sequences of behaviour, but who do not fully understand how to use and apply these skills appropriately. The main emphasis in drama, therefore, is on *refining* these behavioural sequences, rather than on teaching them. Participation in both activities may be enhanced by visual and perceptual discrimination, gross and fine motor control, dexterity, and trust. Drama also requires some degree of flexibility of approach, an understanding of role, and social interaction.

The differences between play and drama are shown in the two example plans. In the first, creative play uses physical and tactile experiences to help in the discovery of words, objects and concepts; in the second example the drama session explores feelings, understanding of role, emotion, dress and action through discussion and role play. In play, learning takes place through the senses, and by relating new experiences to old; in drama, learning occurs through role experimentation. Play is most likely to be part of basic and intermediate timetables, whereas drama is more likely to be found in intermediate and advanced timetables.

Whichever type of group is being run, the activity should take place in a familiar and appropriate environment. Staff participating in the group should be able to model and demonstrate appropriate behaviour, and have both the confidence to take an active role and the enthusiasm to involve clients in the activity. Generally, the more able the group, the less need there is for equipment to reinforce the imaginary input; a leader of a drama group should be able to provide 'props' and 'equipment' by stimulating each person's imagination to the full.

Play and drama, because they are deeply rooted in self-expression and interaction, provide many opportunities for the development of creative skills and spontaneity. However, not every client attending a play or drama group will know how to participate, or have the confidence to join in. Both types of group therefore need to provide a secure and supportive atmosphere, and encourage any level of participation, however small. Groups, and individuals within groups, should gradually be moved towards higher levels of participation and achievement, and, as far as possible, any problems that occur within the group should be dealt with in a way which preserves the atmosphere created.

EXAMPLE GROUP PLAN NO. 4

Activity

Creative play — 'Making jam'.

Group details

Six people + three staff, for approximately 1 hour.

Teaching objectives

(1) Each person will identify basic colours, e.g. red and green.
(2) Each person will participate in simulating the creation of a jar of real jam.
(3) Each person will relate the play sequences to real-life experiences.
(4) Each person will participate in all songs.

Equipment needed

Green sheets to create 'bushes', red shapes for 'raspberries', small bowls/punnets, large saucepan or preserving pan, polystyrene beads for 'sugar', spoons, jam jars, cardboard box, raspberry jam, bread and butter.

Presentation

(1) Encourage each client to look at the pot of raspberry jam. Describe it, let everyone taste it, and talk about how it would

normally be eaten.
(2) Describe the various processes involved — picking the fruit, bringing it home, cooking it in a pan, bottling it, letting it cool and eating it.
(3) Suggest the group 'makes' some jam.

Content

(1) Go out into the garden (i.e. where the green sheets have been draped and covered with red shapes to represent bushes with raspberries on them).
(2) Pick the 'raspberries' off the 'bushes' and put them in the punnets/bowls, singing an appropriate song such as 'This is the way we pick the fruit'.
(3) Take 'fruit' back to the 'house' (i.e. where the group started from), singing suitably adapted songs to fit the actions.
(4) Put the 'fruit' and 'sugar' into the saucepan and stir the 'jam' until it is cooked.
(5) Ladle the cooked 'jam' into jam jars.
(6) Wash up equipment.
(7) Put the newly made 'jam' into the 'cupboard' (improvise with a cardboard box).

Conclusions

(1) Go over main parts of the creative play sequence again.
(2) Identify how jam is eaten.
(3) Take real pot of jam, bread and butter from the 'cupboard' and finish with a sampling session!

EXAMPLE GROUP PLAN NO. 5

Activity

Drama — What happens at a wedding.

Group details

Twenty people with five staff for approximately 1½ hours.

Teaching objectives

(1) Each person will identify someone who might attend a wedding.
(2) Each person will describe the type of clothes worn to a wedding.
(3) Each person will demonstrate appropriate social behaviour for the role-play situation.

(4) Each person will identify something that they should and should not do at a wedding.

(5) Each person will describe something which happens at a wedding.

Equipment needed

Suitable props, e.g. bouquet, rings, confetti, instant picture camera, wedding music, hats.

Presentation

(1) Ask if anyone has been to a wedding, and discuss general details that are already known. If possible look at wedding photographs or videos. Sing songs about weddings.

(2) Discuss why weddings happen, where they happen and who gets married.

(3) Decide how the room needs to be arranged to simulate the environment for the wedding.

Content

(1) Identify the roles that will have to be played, and describe appropriate social behaviour. Discuss and practise the facial expressions and actions that may be associated with each role, e.g. mother of bride crying but happy, father of bride smiling, bridegroom nervous, vicar beaming.

(2) Identify what special clothes individuals would wear, and any special items they might carry. e.g. bouquet.

(3) Discuss what happens to each person at weddings, i.e. guests get dressed, wrap a present, go to church and meet their relatives and friends, sit in the church and wait for the bride, watch the bride walk down the aisle, listen to the wedding service, follow the bride and groom outside the church, photographs and confetti, travel to reception, give presents, eat meal and dance, say goodbye to bride and groom.

(4) Divide the group into (a) the bridal party, (b) family and vicar, (c) wedding guests and (d) photographer. Find suitable props.

(5) Act out wedding role play, taking photographs throughout.

Conclusions

(1) Sit in a circle and discuss the role play, using photographs as tools to prompt opinions and reactions. Discuss appropriate and inappropriate behaviours that occurred.

(2) Summarise main teaching points, then clear away any equipment used.

GAMES

Games activities are useful in providing a slightly more pressured training experience within which social skills can be practised. Without being overly competitive, games activities require clients to, for example, take turns, work with a partner or team towards a common goal, follow rules and cope with winning and losing. Games sessions can be used recreationally, as an educational medium, or as a means of generalising skills learned elsewhere. Different types of games lend themselves to different types of uses.

Board games are very varied in both the level of understanding required and the complexity of the rules. Games can involve simple matching procedures, or require clients to follow complex sets of instructions. Some games can be readily adapted to meet different needs.

Card games tend to require more co-ordination because of the need to hold cards while making decisions and moves, but (particularly if a standard pack of cards is used) card games can be more flexible than any other sort of game. Card games are also played socially, and may therefore help clients to integrate with local community groups.

Team games include all the traditional 'party' games where people have to identify with a group or team, carry out an activity and respond positively to the pressure produced by competition. These games may well include dancing, e.g. in spot-prize games, or elimination dances.

Computer games are increasingly being used to provide a quite different type of educational and recreational experience. The operation of any computer game can be modified using adapted switches and input devices, e.g. joysticks, a concept keyboard, a touch-sensitive screen or suck–blow switches.

EXAMPLE GROUP PLAN NO. 6

Activity

Games afternoon.

Group details

Twenty people + five staff for approximately 1½ hours.

Teaching objectives

(1) Each person will participate in the activities, practising both gross and fine motor skills.
(2) Each person will work appropriately with other group members, and react positively to all competitive results.
(3) Each person will use appropriate descriptive vocabulary throughout the activity.
(4) Each person will demonstrate an understanding of rules and agreed procedures.
(5) Each person will demonstrate an understanding of appropriate types of interaction, and social skills.

Equipment needed

Cassette/record player with sufficient volume to be heard above noise, variety of music, games equipment, prizes, team badges/ markers.

Presentation

(1) Introduce the activity.
(2) Ask clients to request any favourite games, dances or activities.

Content

(1) While music is playing, ask clients to search the room for previously hidden objects/shapes/pictures. Give a small prize to everyone who finds something.
(2) Group dance, e.g. Conga.
(3) Elimination dance.
(4) Pass the parcel.
(5) Balloon dance.
(6) Country dancing.
(7) Horse racing ('horses' heads attached to dustpans, with 50 yards of string tied to the handle and wound around a piece of 2-inch dowelling. Contestants sit at one end of the hall; the string from their 'horse' is unwound until all 'horses' lie on the floor at the opposite end of the hall. The first person to wind his 'horse' from one end of the hall to the other is the winner).
(8) Disco dancing.
(9) Dressing-up races.

(10) Talent spot.
(11) Key race (a key on a piece of string has to be passed through every team member's clothing).

Conclusions

(1) Special requests from clients.
(2) Final dance.

SINGING

Singing is often seen as 'music', but actually meets quite different therapeutic objectives. The key difference lies in the verbalisation needed to participate in singing, which then allows singing to be used to consolidate and develop communication skills, cognitive skill, concept formation, deductive/reasoning skills, socialisation, recognition of mood/feelings, and reminiscence/memory/recall. Participation in this activity may be enhanced by the ability to listen, and to recognise/copy/memorise words, phrases, rhythm and tunes. Individuals do not necessarily need to be able to reproduce the correct pitch to benefit from singing.

Songs can be grouped into related themes and used to illustrate teaching points. For example, group members could have to:

(1) identify songs from listening to the tune (aural discrimination);
(2) name a song that refers to a particular topic, e.g. songs about weather, Christmas, love or holidays (conceptual discrimination);
(3) name a song that includes a certain name or word, e.g. Lily, dog or Johnny (content discrimination);
(4) name a song associated with a certain event, era, or stage in development, e.g. war-time songs, nursery rhymes, national anthem or carols (memory and recall/reminiscence);
(5) name a song associated with a particular mood, emotion or feeling, e.g. happiness, sadness, patriotism or love (discrimination of mood/emotion);
(6) choose a song that they think another group member will like, and say why (interaction/social perception);
(7) choose a song that has special memories for them, and say why (recall/reminiscence);
(8) name a song suggested by a picture, prop or hat, e.g. a soldier's hat, dancing shoes, bread and cheese or various smells, and talk

197

about memories evoked by the object/song (reminiscence and conceptual matching).

Singing also encourages socialisation and the development of interaction skills. Group members need to be able to work together to sing a song, but individual performances can also be used to help group members to listen and compliment someone else, to value their colleagues and to demonstrate socially acceptable methods of showing appreciation. Some aspects of singing also provide a degree of physical activity.

Singing is not necessarily unsuitable for people who are deaf and/or cannot verbally communicate. Careful seating arrangements, the use of microphones or communication equipment, and the use of signing systems to mirror the actual words of the song, can over-come many of the apparent difficulties. Incorporating signing into singing not only allows non-verbal clients to participate, but inform-ally teaches other group members the basic signs that they can then use to communicate with their colleagues.

One fairly essential item for a singing session is a piano (and someone to play it!). Portable organs work well, but pianos tend to give greater clarity of melody, which may be important if group members have problems in hearing or discriminating sound. Guitars again can be useful, but they often need someone with a strong voice leading the singing so that the main tune can be easily recognised. Sessions can be successfully run without an instrument or accom-panist using pre-recorded tapes, but obviously some of the flexibility of having a live accompanist is lost.

EXAMPLE GROUP PLAN NO. 7

Activity

Action singing.

Group details

Ten people + five staff, for approximately 1 hour.

Teaching objectives

(1) Each person will correctly use group members' names.
(2) Each person will identify different body parts, both in response to questions and in relation to the content of songs/poems.
(3) Each person will imitate simple gestures.

Equipment needed

Cassette player and tapes, poems and picture books, song sheets, ball.

Presentation

(1) Introduce the activity.
(2) Ask each client to identify different people in the group by name.
(3) Use ball to reinforce use of names — either ask each client to name a person and throw the ball to him, or name someone and ask the client to throw the ball to that person.

Content

(1) Gentle warm-up exercises to music. Identify different parts of the body during this section.
(2) Read poems aloud and supplement the story with actions. Encourage clients to copy the actions and look at appropriate pictures.
(3) Action singing, using specially recorded music. Encourage clients to sing and perform appropriate actions.
(4) Personal choice — each client chooses a favourite song or rhyme and performs it either individually or with other group members.

Conclusions

(1) Revision of main points of the session.
(2) Special requests.
(3) Short relaxation period.

EXAMPLE GROUP PLAN NO. 8

Activity

Singing (theme = discrimination of sweet, sour/bitter, savoury).

Group details

Fifteen people + three staff for approximately 1½ hours.

Teaching objectives

(1) Each person will demonstrate recognition of themes and conceptual links between songs.
(2) Each person will be able to correctly extract required information from a song.

(3) Each person will correctly select at least one song according to the chosen themes.

(4) Each person will participate fully in the activity.

Equipment needed

Piano, organ, guitar or appropriate cassette tapes, music, song books.

Presentation

(1) Discuss the chosen theme — food tastes. Make sure everyone understands what is meant by sweet, savoury and sour/bitter.

(2) Identify foods that fall into each category.

(3) Explain the forthcoming activity to the group.

Content

(1) Sing general food-related songs, e.g. 'Food, glorious food!', as preparation.

(2) Show a selection of sweet foods, and identify all of them. Taste several of the example foods.

(3) Sing one or two songs that mention sweet foods either in general, or specifically, e.g. 'A spoonful of sugar', or 'You are my honey, honeysuckle'.

(4) Blindfolded tasting of sweet foods.

(5) Teach one new song about sweet foods.

(6) Sing one other familiar song about sweet foods.

(7) Repeat nos (2)–(6) for savoury foods.

(8) Repeat nos (2)–(6) for sour/bitter foods.

Conclusions

(1) Discuss different tastes and recap on the major taste differences.

(2) Ask each person to identify which type of taste he liked best, and to name one food falling into that category.

(3) Finish with two or three general food-related songs.

MUSIC

Music, with the possible exception of art, is one of the widest-ranging activities available, encompassing everything from making a single sound to the production of a musical show, and success is not dependent on verbal interaction or previous experience. The level of participation is so varied that clients of widely differing abilities can successfully work together, although participation may be enhanced by some degree of expressive and receptive ability, motor control, copying and recognition of different sounds, rhythms and melodies.

Obviously some musical projects do require staff to have technical musical knowledge, but for the vast majority of musical sessions the only knowledge needed is recognition of tune, rhythm and metre, and the imagination to use music in a creative manner. Music, though, does not have to be technically perfect to be enjoyable and therapeutic. Music can also be extended into other training activities, e.g. keep-fit sessions; it is a great encourager, and may enhance the participation of clients who would otherwise not join in.

Appreciation of music should always be included. Hearing and responding to music is part of everyday life, but listening in a more specific way, and being able to differentiate between different types of music, may need to be taught and encouraged. Everyone has different musical tastes, and music groups can be used to help clients identify and express their own likes and dislikes more effectively. Listening to music can also be taught as a means of reducing tension and anxiety, and may consequently help some clients to acquire more acceptable ways of dealing with their feelings.

On a more active level, music sessions usually involve a combination of voices and instruments. Music communicates ideas and concepts through sound, and groups can use even the most basic instruments (e.g. spoon, tins, trays, saucepans, filled containers or bottle tops attached to a broomstick), as well as their voices, in developing musical projects. However, if money is available the range of instruments that can be bought is immense. Traditional instruments such as drums, tambourines, bells and maracas provide a flexible, basic set of equipment. A greater variety of experience can be obtained if instruments made from different materials are bought, e.g. wooden drums, bongo drums, a complete drum set, steel drums, tin drums. More unusual or expensive instruments such as hand bells, tubular bells, bird calls and whistles or electronic keyboards, can be added to the basic equipment set at a later stage. Hand chime bells can, nevertheless, be a worthwhile investment because of their versatility. They are tubular steel bells, with a spring-loaded beater attached to their centre, which produce a warm, mellow sound either by flicking the wrist, or by pulling the beater back against its spring, and then letting go. These chime bells can be used for everything from sensory stimulation (because the vibrations can easily be felt) to the formation of chime bell bands, and can be used by anyone. A piano is also a very versatile instrument to have.

201

EXAMPLE GROUP PLAN NO. 9

Activity

Music.

Group details

Twelve clients + three staff for approximately 1½ hours.

Teaching objectives

(1) Each person will identify and demonstrate the concepts of loud/soft, quick/slow, stop/start.
(2) Each person will correctly identify the names of everyone in the group and of all the instruments used (either by name or function).
(3) Each person will use each instrument appropriately.
(4) Each person will co-operate in working with others.
(5) Each person will experiment in producing different sounds.

Equipment needed

Musical instruments, unusual items that make noises, e.g. a bag of marbles, sandpaper and bottles (to blow across the top of the bottle), suitable music, cassette recorder or record player and random method of choice, e.g. spinner, dice or pieces of paper to be drawn from a hat.

Presentation

(1) Sit group in circle and introduce the activity, describing what is going to happen. Ask each client to introduce the person sitting next to him to the group either by giving his name, or indicating the correct name from a choice of two or three.
(2) Sing two or three well-known songs with actions.
(3) Name and demonstrate the pieces of equipment. Talk about the sounds that each one makes.

Content

(1) Each person selects a type of instrument, e.g. one that is blown, beaten or shaken, names it (same procedure as in no. (1) above), and demonstrates how to play it.
(2) Introduction of stop/start. Everyone plays together alternating stop/start in response to the leader.
(3) Introduction of loud/soft. Everyone plays instruments together, alternating loud/soft play in response to cues from the leader.

(4) Introduction of quick/slow. Everyone plays instruments together, alternating quick/slow playing in response to cues from the leader.

(5) Alternative instruments are identified by name. Each person chooses an item, and shows how to use it to make a noise, with the remainder of the group describing that noise in terms of loud, soft, pleasant, unpleasant, etc.

(6) Playing alternative instruments to a piece of music.

(7) Each person randomly selects another type of instrument.

(8) Repeat no. (5) with new instrument.

(9) Repeat no. (6) with new instrument.

(10) Repeat no. (7) with new instrument.

(11) Introduce a short story. Each person how has three instruments to use as sound effect for the story. At each point of the story where sound effects are needed (e.g. wind blowing can be simulated by blowing across a bottle top, thunder by beating a drum, or animals by voice or specialist whistles), clients can volunteer their 'noises'.

Conclusions

(1) Resumé of the work that has been done in the session. Ask clients to describe what they have done.

(2) Everyone chooses the instrument they like best out of the three they have, and the whole group plays together.

(3) Group discussion about favourite noises and instruments.

(4) Instruments returned to the group leader according to name or type.

ART AND CRAFT

Art and craft activities provide the widest range of application of any creative media. In normal development, art-based activity occurs before competence in self-help activities, so art techniques can be adapted to meet the needs of the most profoundly handicapped person. There are many books and magazines giving details of the different media and techniques that are available.

Art and craft are usually paired together, but they are quite different media. Generally, art involves the use of one or two related techniques or processes in the creation of a piece of work, but craft processes usually involve taking materials and either altering or combining them in some way to create a piece of work. Many of the techniques involved in craft work, e.g. cutting, folding and glueing, require intermediate rather than basic level skills.

Art experiences can be clean or dirty, tactile or technical, planned or spontaneous, individual or group-orientated, functional or imaginative. Participation in this activity may be enhanced by (a) some degree of motor control, (b) hand–eye co-ordination and (c) some degree of perceptual skill. Various aids can assist clients with limited physical and visual skills to participate. The range of materials available to work with is huge, with many items that have been prepared with children in mind being ideal for therapeutic experimentation, e.g. gel-like finger paints, and various types and sizes of crayons/pastels/pens. Many art materials can be obtained cheaply through local firms and dealers, and more and more 'scrap' projects are developing where, for a small annual fee, members can take away any paper or collage materials that they find useful or interesting.

EXAMPLE GROUP NO. 10

Activity

Collage.

Group details

Twelve people + four staff for approximately 1½ hours.

Teaching objectives

(1) Each person will correctly demonstrate and use a variety of technical skills, e.g. cutting, glueing, colour matching.
(2) Each person will demonstrate an understanding of theme and the selection of appropriate materials.
(3) Each person will identify relevant aspects of the chosen theme that can be included in the collage.
(4) Each person will demonstrate a conception of form and shape through the construction of the collage.
(5) Each person will identify different qualities, names and textures associated with the various materials used.

Equipment needed

Basic tools, e.g. scissors, paper, glue, and a variety of scrap and craft materials, e.g. material, card, paper, foil.

Presentation

(1) Discuss possible themes. If possible choose a theme related to a recent event, or time of the year, e.g. making a collage about fish after acquiring an aquarium.

(2) Discuss what is relevant to that theme. Ask each person to identify either something different that could be found in, for example, an aquarium, or materials that might be useful in depicting the chosen theme.

(3) Put on aprons/overalls.

Content

(1) Divide the group into four subsections, each with responsibility for constructing part of the overall picture, e.g. (a) fish; (b) plants; (c) rocks; (d) background/water/tank.

(2) Each group creates/constructs a variety of items within their chosen section, and talks about characteristics of their items.

(3) The whole group reassembles, and starts to construct the composite collage.

(4) Those responsible for the background/water/tank tell the rest of the group what they know about water, and then lay out their work ready for the rest of the items to be assembled onto it.

(5) Those responsible for the rocks tell the group what they know, and then decide where to position their 'rocks'.

(6) Repeat no. (5) for the group constructing 'plants'.

(7) Repeat no. (5) for the group constructing 'fish'.

Conclusions

(1) Clear away and wash up while collage dries.

(2) Look at finished work, recap on procedures used, and the different parts of the overall picture.

(3) Display collage on wall.

GARDENING

Gardening (or horticulture) is another creative medium that provides a wide variety of work. The biggest disadvantage of certain projects is the growing time that must elapse before the results are seen. This can be overcome if gardening is a regularly used activity and there are always plants or crops at different stages of growth, but if gardening is only occasionally used, the time from planting to full growth needs to be considered, and matched to the client's needs and abilities. participation in this activity may be enhanced by hand–eye co-ordination, manual dexterity and fine motor manipulation. At more advanced levels, concepts of time passage, sequencing and physical fitness are required.

Access to a garden, and staff with the skills to run a successful horticulture area, obviously make a tremendous difference to any therapeutic programme. Garden areas can become places for leisure and social activities as well as for work, and provide sensory and social experiences, e.g. through 'feely' or 'smelly' gardens, barbecues and fountains.

Therapeutically, gardening can be structured to provide training in a variety of areas such as co-ordination, strength, stamina and precision. The location of the activity tends to determine the degree of social interaction achieved through the work, with indoor activities providing the most flexible settings. Gardening does not necessarily need to involve conventional materials, i.e. soil and seedlings. Very successful groups can be run working on dried flower arrangements, drying and packaging herbs, making gardening equipment, etc. Apart from the initial cost of buying equipment, gardening is usually an inexpensive activity to run; in many cases, where it is used regularly, it is self-financing.

EXAMPLE GROUP PLAN NO. 11

Activity

Dried flower trees.

Group details

Six people + two staff for approximately 1 hour.

Teaching objectives

(1) Each person will identify and match colours.
(2) Each person will manipulate the dried flowers without breaking them.
(3) Each person will demonstrate constructional skills.
(4) Each person will show an understanding of the sequencing of the activity.

Equipment needed

Flower pots or tubs, gravel, pieces of wood/dowelling/sticks, expanded polystyrene shapes, e.g. balls and cones, dried flowers and grasses in different colours, ribbon.

Presentation

(1) Introduce the activity and show a finished article.
(2) Identify the component parts and let each group member look at and feel all materials.
(3) Demonstrate how to choose materials and construct a dried flower tree.

Content

(1) Encourage each member to choose dried flowers and grasses in the colours they want, plus a flower pot or container, a stick and a polystyrene shape.
(2) Hold the stick upright in the flower pot and fill the pot with gravel.
(3) Push the polystyrene shape on to the top of the stick.
(4) Breaking the dried flowers into small pieces, push them into the polystyrene until the whole shape is densely packed with dried material.

Conclusions

(1) Finish each 'tree' off with a ribbon.
(2) Discuss the processes needed to produce the 'trees'.
(3) Look at each person's finished 'tree' and describe it.
(4) Display the finished items.

SALEABLE WORK

Any timetable which included work, or work training, will produce items for sale. The production of these items forms the basic activity upon which work training is structured (work and work training sessions are discussed in more detail in Chapter 8, Advanced Living Skills). Participation in this activity requires concentration, manual dexterity, understanding and implementation of instructions, sequencing skill and perseverance.

Any task which can be broken down into component parts, so that different people can work together to produce a whole item, is relevant. It is preferable to have all component parts of the task under direct control, even if this requires subcontracting certain parts of the whole task to other training centres, and each task should preferably be made up of component parts of varying complexity.

Whatever is produced should, though, be of a high quality, and sale prices may need to take into account a higher than usual rejection level for the goods produced. Various productive tasks can be incorporated into these sessions e.g.:

(1) *Chamois leathers* — chamois leather offcuts can either be sewn into large leathers, or threaded together into hand-sized wash leathers. Threaded leathers can be divided into four basic processes and arranged as follows on a work table, as shown in Figure 10.1.

Figure 10.1

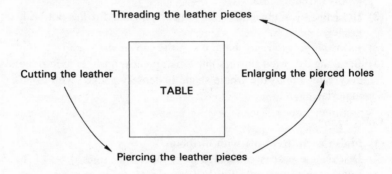

(2) *Printed cards and stationery* — printed material can achieve a high-quality finish and create a range of jobs. Birthday and Christmas cards, and decorated writing paper, can be produced either with a traditional printing press, picture blocks and type, or with a small, commercially available photographic screen printing machine. A screen printing machine is much quicker and easier to set up, and still requires a degree of precision in placing the cards/paper prior to printing, but produces original designs in bright colours very rapidly. Designs can therefore be varied more easily than with a traditional printing press. This type of work also provides folding, sorting, matching, counting, packaging and finishing tasks.

(3) *Wooden items* — a range of wooden goods can be produced, either from commercially available kits or from raw materials. Scrap pieces of wood can be converted into toys or games, e.g. solitaire puzzles; wine racks and novelty clock shapes can be cut

out with a jig saw and then assembled and finished in work groups; kits for making small wooden items such as spice racks can be bought, assembled and sold. Component parts of making wooden items include sanding, sticking/joining, painting, finishing and packaging.

(4) *Dried flowers* — basic materials can be grown and then used during the winter months to produce saleable items. Dried garden produce can be turned into pot pourri, herb sachets, pomanders, dried flower arrangements. Very effective (and very saleable!) dried flower arrangements can be made by virtually anyone, with a flower pot, an attractively shaped twig or branch, spheres of flower arranging foam, dried flowers and colourant sprays.

(5) *Pottery and plaster casts* — producing high-quality pottery is difficult to achieve using clay, but slip moulds and moulds for casting in plaster make it much easier to produce consistently good results. Obviously slip (i.e. liquid clay) still requires firing and glazing in a kiln, but if a kiln is unavailable, a variety of items, e.g. chess sets, can be made from plaster which only need to be painted and varnished when dry. If harder work is required, concrete can be cast in moulds to produce garden brickwork.

(6) *Preserves* — if a fruit garden is available, producing a range of jams, preserves and chutneys can be an appropriate work project. Microwave ovens can reduce much of the cooking time and make it easier for a greater range of people to participate. This activity also involves a lot of preparation of the fruit and equipment, labelling, sealing and packaging for sale.

(7) *Sale of food* — this can be a useful occasional project, particularly in a maintenance timetable. Lunch-time snacks can be produced and sold within the same session, giving clients a range of tasks from food preparation to setting suitable prices, selling goods, and working out the amount of money made.

(8) *Gardening* — the range of gardening work available is extensive, but heavy outdoor work is often limited to the fittest, most able people. Indoor work projects can produce different pot plants, fresh and dried herbs, bulb bowls, and so on, although a heated greenhouse makes a wider variety of projects possible. Gardening is an activity that can provide something for everyone, despite disabilities, and is pleasurable as well as productive.

In practice, any session producing saleable work will have a variety of work being carried out at any one time. However, the basic structure of the group will remain the same.

EXAMPLE GROUP NO. 12

Activity

Work training.

Group details

Sixteen people with four staff for approximately 1½ hours.

Teaching objectives

(1) Each person will demonstrate a range of appropriate work behaviours.
(2) Each person will work consistently to reach a target production level.
(3) Each person will share equipment, and demonstrate co-operation with colleagues.
(4) Each person will change jobs whenever necessary.

Equipment needed

Dependent on the work tasks included in the session.

Presentation

(1) Review results of previous work session and set tentative work targets for current session.
(2) Explain current tasks and divide work amongst the group.

Content

(1) Check that each person knows what he is doing, and has the correct equipment/materials.
(2) Clients work through current projects, using staff as supervisors who can provide advice, encouragement and more work.

Conclusions

(1) Group members review the amount of work that has been achieved, both overall and by individual group members.
(2) Group members put away materials/equipment and leave room tidy.

SUMMARY

Many, many creative media are available to be used therapeutically to help develop living skills, some of which are described in this chapter. The advantage of using creative media is lost, though, if activities are too repetitive, or fail to stimulate the interest of the client group. Any training timetable that uses these media therefore needs to be innovative and adaptable, and always ready to experiment.

Further information

Music

J. Alvin, *Music for the Handicapped Child* (Oxford University Press, Oxford, 1977).

P. Smith and D. Wheatley, *Things to Sing/Silly Things to Sing/Christmas Things to Sing* (E.J. Arnold Ltd, London, 1976).

M. Wood, *Music for Living* (British Institute for Mental Handicap, Kidderminster, 1982).

Movement

B. Brosnan, *Yoga for Handicapped People* (Souvenir Press, London, 1982).

G. Levete, *No Handicap to Dance* (Souvenir Press, London, 1982).

Physical exercise

S.J. George and B. Hart, *Physical Education for Handicapped Children* (Souvenir Press, London, 1983).

L. Groves, *Physical Education for Special Needs* (Cambridge University Press, Cambridge, 1979).

K. Latto, *Give Us the Chance — sport and physical recreation for the mentally handicapped* (Disabled Living Foundation, 1981).

S. Moule *et al.*, *Educational Rhythmics in Practice — starting and running a programme with the mentally handicapped* (British Institute of Mental Handicap, Kidderminster, 1984).

Play and drama

C. Astell-Burt, *Puppetry for the Mentally Handicapped* (Souvenir Press, London, 1981).

J. Comins *et al.*, *Activities and Ideas* (Winslow Press, London, 1983).

S. Jennings (ed.), *Dramatherapy: theory and practice for teachers and clinicians* (Croom Helm, London/Brookline Books, Cambridge, Massachusetts, 1987).

S. Jennings, *Remedial Drama* (Pitman, London, 1978).

F. Mercer, *Handbook of Indoor Social Activities* (Winslow Press, London, 1981).

A.J. Remocker and E.T. Storch, *Action Speaks Louder: a handbook of non-verbal group techniques* (Churchill Livingstone, Edinburgh and New York, 1982).

B. Warren (ed.), *Using the Creative Arts in Therapy* (Croom Helm, London/Brookline Books, Cambridge, Massachusetts, 1984).

Cooking

R. Marshall, *My Cookbook* (British Institute of Mental Handicap, Kidderminster, 1983).

G. Conacher, *Kitchen Sense for Disabled People* (Croom Helm, London and New York, 1986).

Art and craft

S.M. Atack, *Art Activities for the Handicapped* (Souvenir Press, London, 1980).

M. Bennett *et al.*, *Jewellery Anyone Can Make* (Collins, London, 1974).

T. Dalley, *Art as Therapy* (Tavistock Publications, London and New York, 1984).

E. French and S. Schrapel *Tie-dying and Fabric Printing* (Robert Hale, London, 1972).

F. Law, *Things to Make from Card* (Collins, London, 1974).

F. Law, *Things to Make from Junk* (Collins, London, 1974).

M. Liebmann, *Art Therapy for Groups* (Croom Helm, London/Brookline Books, Cambridge, Massachusetts, 1986).

J. Robertson, *Practical Art Techniques* (Winslow Press, London, 1983).

Gardening

A. Cloet and C. Underhill, *Gardening Is for Everyone* (Souvenir Press, London, 1982).

P. Elliott, *The Garden and the Handicapped Child* (Disabled Living Foundation, London, 1978).

Games

M. Cotton, *Out of Doors with Handicapped People* (Souvenir Press, London, 1981).

M. Cotton, *Outdoor Adventures for Handicapped People* (Souvenir Press, London, 1983).

N. Croucher, *Outdoor Pursuits for Handicapped People* (Woodhead-Faulkner, Cambridge, 1981).

General

G. Levete, *et al.*, *The Creative Tree* (Michael Russell, Salisbury, 1987).

Selected Further Reading

Texts marked with an asterisk (*) refer to the use of aids and equipment, and techniques for managing physical disability.

Banus, B.S. *et al.*, *The Developmental Therapist* (Slack Inc., Thorofare, N.J. 1979).

Bleck, E.E., *Orthopaedic Management of Cerebral Palsy* (W.B. Saunders, Philadelphia, 1979).

Bowley, A.H. and Gardner, L., *The Handicapped Child* (Churchill Livingstone, Edinburgh and New York, 1981).

Clarke, A.M. *et al.*, *Mental Deficiency — the changing outlook* (Methuen, London and New York, 1985).

Clarke, D., *Mentally Handicapped People: living and learning* (Baillière Tindall, Eastbourne and Philadelphia, 1982).

Clarke, P.N. and Allen, A.S., *Occupational Therapy for Children* (C.V. Mosby Co., St Louis, 1985).

Copeland, M. *et al.*, *Occupational Therapy for Mentally Retarded Children* (University Park Press, Baltimore, 1976).

Cottam, P. and Sutton, A., *Conductive Education: a system for overcoming motor disorders* (Croom Helm, London and New York, 1985).

Craft, M. *et al.*, *Mental Handicap: a multidisciplinary approach* (Baillière Tindall, Eastbourne and Philadelphia, 1985).

Darnborough, A. and Kinrade, D., *Directory for the Disabled* (Woodhead Faulkner, Cambridge, 1981).

*Disabled Living Foundation Information Sheets, *Aids and Equipment* (Obtainable from DLF, 380–384 Harrow Road, London W9 2HU).

Drillien, C.M. and Drummond, M.B., *Neuro-developmental Problems in Early Childhood: assessment and management* (Blackwell Scientific, Oxford, 1978).

Ellis, D. (ed.), *Sensory Impairment in Mentally Handicapped People* (Croom Helm, London/College-Hill Press, San Diego, California, 1986).

*Equipment for the Disabled, Booklets on wheelchairs, communication, clothing and dressing, home management, disabled mothers, personal care, leisure and gardening, housing and furniture, hoists, walking aids, disabled children, and outdoor transport (Available from 2 Foredown Drive, Portslade, Brighton N4 2BB).

Gesell, A., *The First Five Years of Life* (Methuen, London and New York, 1966).

Hilgard, E.R. *et al.*, *Introduction to Psychology* (Harcourt Brace Jovanovitch, New York, 1979).

Hopkins, H.L. and Smith, H.D., *Willards and Spackman Occupational Therapy* (J.B. Lippincott Co., Philadelphia, Pennsylvania, 1983).

Illingworth, R.S., *The Normal Child — some problems of the early years and their treatment* (Churchill Livingstone, Edinburgh and New York, 1985).

Illingworth, R.S., *The Development of the Infant and Young Child* (Churchill Livingstone, Edinburgh and New York, 1985).

*Jay, P., *Coping with Disability* (Disabled Living Foundation, London, 1984).

Lederman, E.F., *Occupational Therapy in Mental Retardation* (Charles C. Thomas, Springfield, Illinois, 1984).

Malin, N., Race, D. and Jones, G., *Services for the Mentally Handicapped in Britain* (Croom Helm, London, 1980).

Murphy, G. and Wilson, B., *Self Injurious Behaviour* (British Institute of Mental Handicap, Kidderminster, 1985).

Panckhurst, J., *Focus on Physical Handicap — provision for young people with special needs in further education* (NFER-Nelson, Windsor, 1980).

Russell, D., *Mental Handicap* (Churchill Livingstone, Edinburgh and New York, 1985).

Sines, O. and Bicknell, J., *Caring for Mentally Handicapped People in the Community* (Harper & Row, London and New York, 1985).

Turner, A., *The Practice of Occupational Therapy* (Churchill Livingstone, Edinburgh and New York, 1981).

Wilson, M., *Occupational Therapy in Long-Term Psychiatry* (Churchill Livingstone, Edinburgh and New York, 1983).

Wilson, M., *Occupational Therapy in Short-Term Psychiatry* (Churchill Livingstone, Edinburgh and New York, 1984).

Index

Entries including capital letters indicate reference either to currently available assessments, or to specific resources.